THE FOUNDING DEBATE

WHERE SHOULD THE POWER OVER OUR LIVES RESIDE?

MATT A. MAYER

TWITTER: @OHIOMATT

FACEBOOK: WWW.FACEBOOK.COM/LIBERTYFOUND

WWW.LIBERTYFOUND.ORG

PROVISUM STRATEGIES LLC

Other Books by Matt A. Mayer

HOMELAND SECURITY AND FEDERALISM: *PROTECTING AMERICA FROM OUTSIDE THE BELTWAY (WITH FOREWARD BY THE HONORABLE EDWIN MEESE III)*

TAXPAYERS DON'T STAND A CHANCE: *HOW BATTLEGROUND OHIO LOSES NO MATTER WHO WINS (AND WHAT TO DO ABOUT IT)*

Provisum Strategies LLC
P.O. Box 98
Dublin, Ohio 43017-0098

First Provisum Strategies LLC edition December 2013

For information about special discounts for bulk purchases, please contact Provisum Strategies at checkmate@provisumstrategies.com.

Cover Designed by John Fleming

Manufactured in the United States of America

Library of Congress Cataloguing-in-Publication Data is available.

ISBN-13: 978-1493726714

ISBN-10: 1493726714

This book is dedicated to my ancestors who came from Germany beginning in the early 1800s to secure a better life for themselves and their progeny. I especially dedicate this book to my grandfather Bernard F. Kroger.

CONTENTS

THE FOUNDING DEBATE

1

FRAMING THE DEBATE

The scene is a familiar one. You've seen it portrayed in paintings and pictures in history books and on television. It is the summer of 1787. America's Founding Fathers are gathered in Philadelphia to repair the deficiencies of the Articles of Confederation. Instead of repairing the Articles of Confederation, they draft and propose a new Constitution.

Upon adopting the Constitution on September 17, 1787, they submitted it to the thirteen states for ratification. Over the next eighteen months, a vigorous debate occurred over the proposed Constitution. In September 1789, Congress proposed the Bill of Rights, which were the first ten ratified amendments to the Constitution modeled after the English Bill of Rights contained in the Magna Carta.

During the debate over the Constitution, two sets of men took their debate to the newspapers (their version of the airwaves). On one side were the Federalists, with Alexander Hamilton (future Secretary of the Treasury) and James Madison (future President of the United States) leading the charge. On the other side were the Anti-Federalists, including Robert Yates (future Chief Justice of the New York Supreme Court) and Samuel Bryan (future Comptroller General of Pennsylvania). All of these men wrote using pseudonyms (Publius, Brutus, Centinel, and Old Whig), and all were distinguished and learned men.

One area of their debate focused on the powers of the new federal government under Section 8 of Article I. Specifically, the two sides portrayed drastically different versions of the federal government under Section 8. The Federalist casually dismissed concerns that the federal government would overpower the states. As Hamilton stated in *Federalist No. 31* in what might be two of the most creative sentences written in American history:

> The moment we launch into conjectures about the usurpations of the federal government, we get into an unfathomable abyss, and fairly put ourselves out of the reach of all reasoning. Imagination may range at pleasure till it gets bewildered amidst the labyrinths of an enchanted castle, and knows not on which side to turn to extricate itself from the perplexities into which it has so rashly adventured.

In contrast, the Anti-Federalists warned that the federal government could abolish state legislatures with its new powers. Yates ominously wrote in *Letter V* in Letters of Centinel:

> The legislative power granted for these sections is so unlimited in its nature, may be so comprehensive and boundless in its exercise, that this alone would be amply sufficient to carry the coup de grace to the state governments, to swallow them up in the grand vortex of general empire.

So which end-state would America find itself under the proposed Constitution—a comfortable symbiotic relationship between the federal government and the states where only the fringes get bewildered amidst the labyrinths of an enchanted castle or a federal government that has swallowed the states in a grand vortex of general empire?

A key topic of concern for the Anti-Federalists was the "necessary and proper" language in Section 8. Why did this language worry them? Because, along with what became known as Article V's Supremacy Clause in which federal law trumps state laws, they believed this broad language gave the federal government unfettered power to do whatever it deemed necessary and proper to execute the enumerated powers granted it under the Constitution. Many Americans today view the federal government as the permanent behemoth whose shadow eclipses the sunshine of the states. They've never known an America where it wasn't so encompassing.

How did today's federal government come to be so pervasive in our daily lives? One of the primary vehicles used to achieve the dominance of the federal government was the Necessary and Proper Clause as it related to Section 8's enumerated power of regulating commerce among the several states (the Commerce Clause). So, where did this little phrase come from?

As Juliana Gisela Dalotto details in her comment "American State Constitutions of 1776-1787: The Antecedents of the Necessary [and Proper] Clause" in the *Journal of Constitutional Law* (Vol. 14:5; pages 1326-1332), the group charged with drafting the pertinent section, the Committee of Detail, introduced the Necessary and Proper Clause after several drafts of the section for the new Constitution. As Dalotto notes, Edmund Randolph's "modified version" of the draft first added the "Necessary Clause." Later, James Wilson added the "proprietary" component in the fifth version of the draft.

The final version of the combined Necessary and Proper Clause is contained in the final draft that the Committee of Detail presented to the Constitutional Convention. Unfortunately, the Committee of Detail did not keep records of their debates, so we have no way to know <u>why</u> the Necessary and Proper Clause was added.

Even more problematic, as Randy Barnett notes in his law review article "The Original Meaning of the Necessary and Proper Clause" in the *Journal of Constitutional Law* (Vol. 6:2; pages 185-197), the Constitutional Convention did not debate the Necessary and Proper Clause during the process of adopting the Constitution. In his law review article, Barnett highlights a later debate between Madison and Hamilton on the creation of a national bank in 1791 under the Necessary and Proper Clause.

Barnett quotes Madison arguing that "necessary means necessary"— the federal government could only do what was necessary and proper as it related to an enumerated power, meaning it could not create a national bank as a necessary and proper action under its enumerated power to borrow money. As Madison noted, "If implications, thus remote and thus multiplied, can be linked together, a chain may be formed that will reach every object of legislation, every object within the whole compass of political economy."

Madison made a similar argument during the debate on the Constitution when he noted in *Federalist No. 44*: "No axiom is more clearly established in law, or in reason, than that wherever the end is required, the means are authorized; wherever a general power to do a thing is given, every particular power necessary for doing it is included." For Madison, the particular *necessary* power had to *properly* flow from the general power.

Barnett notes that Hamilton, chief proponent of the national bank, buckled under such a restrictive interpretation of the Necessary and

Proper Clause. He argued "necessary means convenient." Specifically, Hamilton wrote:

> [N]ecessary often means no more than needful, requisite, incidental, useful, or conducive to. It is a common mode of expression to say, that it is necessary for a government or a person to do this or that thing, when nothing more is intended or understood than that the interest of the Government or person require, or will be promoted by, the doing of this or that thing.

Hamilton urged a "liberal latitude to the exercise of the specified powers."

Hamilton's view on the Necessary and Proper Clause also did not change much from 1787 to 1791. In *Federalist No. 33*, Hamilton stated: "The declaration itself, though it may be chargeable with tautology and redundancy, is at least perfectly harmless."

One of the arguments Hamilton made in *The Federalist Papers* to convince citizens that the new constitutional powers of the federal government would not invade the power of the states is that the states held most of the power over citizens' lives. In *Federalist No. 34*, Hamilton argued:

> As this [the power of taxation] leaves open to the States far the greatest part of the resources of the community, there can be no color for the assertion that they would not possess means as abundant as could be desired for the supply of their own wants, independent of all external control. That the field is sufficiently wide will more fully appear when we come to advert to the inconsiderable share of the public expenses for which it will fall to the lot of the State governments to provide.
>
> ...
>
> In pursuing this inquiry, we must bear in mind that we are not to confine our view to the present period, but to look forward to remote futurity. Constitutions of civil government are not to be framed upon a calculation of existing exigencies, but upon a combination of these with the probable exigencies of ages, according to the natural and tried course of human affairs.

So, how did history bear out Hamilton's assertion? The 2013 fiscal year federal budget totalled roughly $3.8 trillion. In contrast, the 2012 fiscal year total for all fifty states (the latest year available) ran to $1.15 trillion—just over 30 percent of the federal budget.

To bolster his argument, Hamilton opined:

> The expenses arising from those institutions which are relative to the mere domestic police of a state, to the support of its legislative, executive, and judicial departments, with their different appendages, and to the encouragement of agriculture and manufactures (which will comprehend almost all the objects of state expenditure), are insignificant in comparison with those which relate to the national defense.

Madison held a similar view. He noted in *Federalist No. 45*, "The operations of the federal government will be most extensive and important in times of war and danger; those of the State governments, in times of peace and security." In the latest federal budget, Congress appropriated $670 billion for defense, which equates to roughly 19 percent of the federal budget. Congress doled out $802 billion for Medicare and Medicaid (23 percent), $768 billion for Social Security (22 percent), and $1,076 trillion for other discretionary federal spending (30 percent), which included $223 billion for interest on the national debt (6 percent).

How did Hamilton and Madison get this so wrong? Recall one of Madison's most famous statements in *Federalist No. 45* where he declared:

> The powers delegated by the proposed Constitution to the federal government, are few and defined. Those which are to remain in the State governments are numerous and indefinite. The former will be exercised principally on external objects, as war, peace, negotiation, and foreign commerce; with which last the power of taxation will, for the most part, be connected. The powers reserved to the several States will extend to all the objects which, in the ordinary course of affairs, concern the lives, liberties, and properties of the people, and the internal order, improvement, and prosperity of the State.

Anti-Federalist Bryan saw things a bit differently. In Centinel's *Letter V*, he warned citizens:

> Whatever law congress may deem necessary and proper for carrying into execution any of the powers vested in

them, may be enacted; and by virtue of this clause, they may controul and abrogate any and every of the laws of the state governments, on the allegation that they interfere with the execution of any of their powers, and yet these laws will "be made in pursuance of the constitution," and of course will "be the supreme law of the land, and the judges in every state shall be bound thereby, any thing in the constitution or laws of any state to the contrary notwithstanding."

There is no reservation made in the whole of this plan in favor of the rights of the separate states.

By zeroing in on the combined one-two punch of the Necessary and Proper Clause with the Supremacy Clause, Bryan foresaw where things could go over the course of time.

The Old Whig joined Bryan in *Essay IV* noting, "Power is very easily increased; indeed it naturally grows in every government; but it hardly ever lessens...I venture to pronounce that those who indulge such hopes [that Congress will exercise power with moderation], are not acquainted with the principles of human nature." In Brutus's *Essay I*, Yates concluded, "[I]t is a truth confirmed by the unerring experience of ages, that every man, and every body of men, invested with power, are ever disposed to increase it, and to acquire a superiority over every thing that stands in their way."

As the debate raged on, the Anti-Federalists called for a Bill of Rights to protect the states and the citizens from the new federal government. Without a Bill of Rights, as the Old Whig pointed out in *Essay II*, "The Congress shall judge of what is necessary and proper in all these cases and in all other cases;—in short in all cases whatsoever. Where then is the restraint?" Yates echoed this sentiment in Brutus's *Essay XII*: "But if this equitable mode of construction [that Congress held express and implied powers] is applied to this part of the constitution; nothing can stand before it." The Anti-Federalists demanded a Bill of Rights to "secure the people their liberties."

We know only two years after the Constitutional Convention adopted the Constitution that Congress passed ten amendments that became our Bill of Rights. The citizens wanted certain rights expressly stated—like the freedom of the press, the freedom of religion, and the right to bear arms. Equally important, with the addition of the Ninth Amendment and Tenth Amendment, the Bill of Rights explicitly stated that the states and the people possessed more rights than those stated in the

Constitution and the corollary restriction that the federal government's powers were limited to those enumerated in the Constitution.

Even with the Bill of Rights, however, the federal government's powers in reality would be limited only by the judiciary's interpretation of the Constitution on words like those in the Necessary and Proper Clause. In fact, the Federalists pointed to the judiciary—the least dangerous branch—as one of the key protectors of state sovereignty and individual liberty.

Yates responded in force by noting in Brutus's *Essay I* that the power of judicial interpretation "will enable them to mould the government, into almost any shape they please." In Brutus's *Essay XII*, Yates added:

> But it is easy to see, that in their adjudications they may establish certain principles, which being received by the legislature, will enlarge their sphere of their power beyond all bounds.
>
> ...
>
> What the principles are, which the court will adopt, it is impossible for us to say...it is not difficult to see, that they may, and probably will, be very liberal ones. We have seen, that they will be authorized to give the constitution a construction according to its spirit and reason, and not to confine themselves to its letter.

Yates clearly predicted the rise of "emanations and penumbras" 177 years later in *Griswold v. Connecticut.*

Over our 226 years history, the Supreme Court issued many decisions on the extent of federal powers as those powers relate to state and individual liberty. In *McCulloch v. Maryland* in 1819, the Supreme Court adopted Hamilton's view that necessary meant convenient. Five years later in *Gibbon v. Ogden*, the Supreme Court made it clear that the Supremacy Clause unequivocally meant federal laws trump state laws. Those cases, however, did not mean that the federal government would do anything it pleased.

One early example is the failed attempt by the federal government to provide disaster relief in 1887 for a drought in Texas. Congress had passed the Texas Seed Act in 1887 that would have given seeds to farmers. In response, as recorded in the 1887 *Congressional Record* (49th Cong., 2d Sess.; Vol. XVIII, Pt. II; 1875), President Grover Cleveland vetoed the legislation noting:

I can find no warrant for such an appropriation in the Constitution; and I do not believe that the power and duty of the General Government ought to be extended to the relief of individual suffering which is in no manner properly related to the public service or benefit. A prevalent tendency to disregard the limited mission of this power and duty should, I think, be steadily resisted, to the end that the lesson should be constantly enforced that, though the people support the Government, the Government should not support the people.

President Cleveland believed that federal action "encourages the expectation of paternal care...and weakens the sturdiness of our national character," and he appealed to the charity of fellow Americans to aid their neighbors in need, which in fact occurred.

Later, during the height of the Depression in 1935, in *A.L.A. Schechter Poultry Corp. v. United States,* the Supreme Court rejected Congress's authority to regulate prices and wages via the National Industrial Recovery Act. The Supreme Court held:

But the authority of the federal government may not be pushed to such an extreme as to destroy the distinction, which the commerce clause itself establishes, between commerce "among the several States" and the internal concerns of a State. The same answer must be made to the contention that is based upon the serious economic situation which led to the passage of the Recovery Act -- the fall in prices, the decline in wages and employment, and the curtailment of the market for commodities. Stress is laid upon the great importance of maintaining wage distributions which would provide the necessary stimulus in starting "the cumulative forces making for expanding commercial activity." Without in any way disparaging this motive, it is enough to say that the recuperative efforts of the federal government must be made in a manner consistent with the authority granted by the Constitution.

Unfortunately, faced with President Franklin D. Roosevelt's 1936 election threat to pack the Supreme Court with new appointees who favoured his progressive views, the Supreme Court wilted only two years after the *Schechter Poultry* decision when it upheld the National Labor Relations Act. Over the next sixty years, the Supreme Court found virtually every expansion of federal power to be proper under the Constitution.

Within a decade of President Ronald Reagan's appointment of individuals to the Supreme Court who believed in interpreting the Constitution based on the letter, not the spirit, of the law, the accretion of federal power slowed. Federal power has not, unfortunately, been reversed in any meaningful manner. Even worse, with the rise of the administrative state since 1937, our lives and livelihoods are increasingly governed, not by specific laws passed by Congress, but by unelected and unaccountable regulatory bodies to which Congress has delegated enormous swaths of unchecked powers.

The best and most recent example is the Patient Protection and Affordable Care Act (Obamacare). The law itself is a 2,000-page giant largely impenetrable to Main Street Americans (and virtually everyone in Washington, D.C.). Former Speaker of the House Nancy Pelosi's infamous statement that they had to pass the bill to know what was in it has proved to be a brilliant summation, regardless of its public relations deficiencies. Americans are just beginning to learn that the legislation passed by Congress is the least of their problems.

When it comes to Obamacare, the thousands of regulations being developed by bureaucrats to give Obamacare its full effect compound the deficiencies and invasiveness of the legislation. The 2,000-page bill will end up being joined by tens of thousands of pages of mandates, regulations, and rules. For example, according to the Competitive Enterprise Institute (CEI), 3,186 final rules have been added in 2013, pushing the 2013 *Federal Register* to more than 77,000 pages, which is just 4,000 pages shy of the 2010 single-year record. CEI estimates the compliance cost for 2013 is between $6.5 billion and $11.8 billion for businesses.

Though the Supreme Court did erroneously uphold Obamacare, it did so under Congress's power to tax, not under the Necessary and Proper Clause. Importantly, in *N.F.I.B. v. Sebelius*, the Supreme Court held:

> Construing the Commerce Clause to permit Congress to regulate individuals precisely because they are doing nothing would open a new and potentially vast domain to congressional authority. Every day individuals do not do an infinite number of things. In some cases they decide not to do something; in others they simply fail to do it. Allowing Congress to justify federal regulation by pointing to the effect of inaction on commerce would

bring countless decisions an individual could potentially make within the scope of federal regulation, and—under the Government's theory—empower Congress to make those decisions for him.

…

Under the Government's logic, that authorizes Congress to use its commerce power to compel citizens to act as the Government would have them act. That is not the country the Framers of our Constitution envisioned.

…

The Commerce Clause is not a general license to regulate an individual from cradle to grave, simply because he will predictably engage in particular transactions. Any police power to regulate individuals as such, as opposed to their activities, remains vested in the States.

Where does that leave us? Legally speaking, we are somewhere between the federal government having the power to regulate the home growing and consumption of food to the federal government not having the power to compel commerce (though it can so long as it frames it as a tax?). Does the gap between these two poles leave much sovereignty for states and individuals to celebrate? That is for each of us to decide.

Obamacare does present a vivid illustration of the debate begun 226 years ago. With the sheer confusion over the implementation of the law and the failures evidenced by the Obamacare website, Hamilton's *Federalist No. 31* flowery dismissal of the Anti-Federalists' imaginations getting lost "amidst the labyrinths of an enchanted castle" isn't as funny as originally intended.

Similarly, with Medicaid already being known as the Pac-Man of state budgets, Obamacare's Medicaid expansion makes Yates' ominous warning in Centinel *Letter V* that the seemingly unlimited power of the federal government could completely overwhelm the states somewhat more credible. Congress has not abolished state legislatures, but do all of its various laws, mandates, regulations, and rules that govern so many domestic issues result in a *de facto* abolishment of state legislatures as mere fiddlers of federal strings?

To help you understand this key founding debate, I have reviewed the founding documents to find the core arguments on each side. In addition to the Constitution, this book contains the five best arguments presented by the Federalists (Hamilton and Madison), the five best arguments presented by the Anti-Federalists (Yates, Bryan, and the unknown "Old Whig"), the Bill of Rights, and select quotes from the ten most relevant U.S. Supreme Court cases decided over the last two hundred years that interpreted the words debated so robustly by our Founding Fathers. With this material, you can read their words for yourself in a couple of hours to come to your own conclusions on who was right, who was wrong, and where things stand today.

No matter where your ideology rests along the clamshell shape of the political spectrum, it seems fairly clear that the locus of power over our lives resides in Washington, D.C., not in the fifty state capitals. You may believe that was a necessary and proper outcome. Many Americans would respectfully disagree.

As I wrote in "Competitive Federalism: Leveraging the Constitution to Rebuild America,"

> The broad brushstrokes of unconstrained federal power perpetually inhibits states from solving America's toughest challenges. Federal laws, rules, and regulations constrain states from freely acting on virtually every subject matter. One-size-fits all policies render meaningful competition among the states limited to few issues.
>
> ...
>
> [C]ompetition energizes us. America's greatness comes from a competitive spirit that is woven into the very DNA of the Constitution. By encouraging competition among the states and between the states and the federal government, our Founding Fathers guaranteed the ultimate success of America, as failure in one state couldn't doom the entire country and state successes could be adopted and tailored by other states. We can solve our complex problems in an iterative process as states learned from and built upon the lessons emanating from the fifty laboratories of competition across the United States.

With the dysfunction in Washington, D.C., and mounting failures produced by the federal government's one-size-fits-all mentality, we must escape the sloth of the centralization status quo. Perhaps the pathway to America's future prosperity is to look to a principle from the past. Competitive federalism was a central doctrine powerfully espoused by the less famous Anti-Federalist Founding Fathers.

It is time the states seized back the right to make decisions about the vast majority of domestic issues in the lives of their citizens. Governors and state legislators from the Left and the Right simply don't need Washington, D.C. to tell them how best to help vulnerable populations, to educate their kids, to maintain and expand their transportation infrastructure, or to improve their citizens' lives on countless other issues. States need to keep their citizens' money that now flows to the federal government and retain the power they held and believed they did not relinquish upon ratifying the Constitution.

By balancing the ability of their citizens to pay with the requirements of necessary government services, the fifty laboratories of competition will solve our toughest challenges with innovation and the nuance demanded by the demographic differences among the states. With fifty governors and legislatures, we will rapidly discover which solutions work and which ones don't work, thereby allowing all states to leverage tested and successful elements from across the United States. This race to the top will ensure that all boats rise instead of fifty boats being weighed down by the federal anchor of laws, mandates, regulations, and rules.

The Liberty Foundation of America is leading the charge to free states to solve problems by way of its Competitive Federalism Project. I hope you consider joining this critical effort. If you can, send an email to your U.S. Senator, U.S. Representatives, State Senator, State Representative, and state-wide elected officials asking them to join this effort. For more information, please visit www.libertyfound.org.

Our Founding Fathers didn't debate some esoteric issue high in the ivory tower of academia. The sheer volume of their writings on the proposed Constitution, which was only 4,400 words, shows how important it was to understand what each word or phrase meant. Our Founding Fathers jousted over the new federal powers in the Constitution during the fragile time when states decided whether or not to ratify it. The fate of our country hung in the balance. With 226 years of history behind us, that debate and its outcome in the future are as relevant and consequential as ever.

I hope you agree.

2

UNITED STATES CONSTITUTION
SEPTEMBER 17, 1787

We the People of the United States, in Order to form a more perfect Union, establish Justice, insure domestic Tranquility, provide for the common defence, promote the general Welfare, and secure the Blessings of Liberty to ourselves and our Posterity, do ordain and establish this Constitution for the United States of America.

ARTICLE I

SECTION 1. All legislative Powers herein granted shall be vested in a Congress of the United States, which shall consist of a Senate and House of Representatives.

SECTION 2. The House of Representatives shall be composed of Members chosen every second Year by the People of the several States, and the Electors in each State shall have the Qualifications requisite for Electors of the most numerous Branch of the State Legislature.

No Person shall be a Representative who shall not have attained to the Age of twenty five Years, and been seven Years a Citizen of the United States, and who shall not, when elected, be an Inhabitant of that State in which he shall be chosen.

Representatives and direct Taxes shall be apportioned among the several States which may be included within this Union, according to their respective Numbers, which shall be determined by adding to the whole Number of free Persons, including those bound to Service for a Term of Years, and excluding Indians not taxed, three fifths of all other Persons. The actual Enumeration shall be made within three Years after the first Meeting of the Congress of the United States, and within every subsequent Term of ten Years, in such Manner as they shall by Law direct. The Number of Representatives shall not exceed one for every thirty Thousand, but each State shall have at Least one Representative; and until such enumeration shall be made, the State of New Hampshire shall be entitled to chuse three, Massachusetts eight, Rhode-Island and Providence Plantations one, Connecticut five, New-York six, New Jersey four, Pennsylvania eight, Delaware one, Maryland six, Virginia ten, North Carolina five, South Carolina five, and Georgia three.

When vacancies happen in the Representation from any State, the Executive Authority thereof shall issue Writs of Election to fill such Vacancies.

The House of Representatives shall chuse their Speaker and other Officers; and shall have the sole Power of Impeachment.

SECTION 3. The Senate of the United States shall be composed of two Senators from each State, chosen by the Legislature thereof, for six Years; and each Senator shall have one Vote.

Immediately after they shall be assembled in Consequence of the first Election, they shall be divided as equally as may be into three Classes. The Seats of the Senators of the first Class shall be vacated at the Expiration of the second Year, of the second Class at the Expiration of the fourth Year, and of the third Class at the Expiration of the sixth Year, so that one third may be chosen every second Year; and if Vacancies happen by Resignation, or otherwise, during the Recess of the Legislature of any State, the Executive thereof may make temporary Appointments until the next Meeting of the Legislature, which shall then fill such Vacancies.

No Person shall be a Senator who shall not have attained to the Age of thirty Years, and been nine Years a Citizen of the United States, and who shall not, when elected, be an Inhabitant of that State for which he shall be chosen.

The Vice President of the United States shall be President of the Senate, but shall have no Vote, unless they be equally divided.

The Senate shall chuse their other Officers, and also a President pro tempore, in the Absence of the Vice President, or when he shall exercise the Office of President of the United States.

The Senate shall have the sole Power to try all Impeachments. When sitting for that Purpose, they shall be on Oath or Affirmation. When the President of the United States is tried, the Chief Justice shall preside: And no Person shall be convicted without the Concurrence of two thirds of the Members present.

Judgment in Cases of Impeachment shall not extend further than to removal from Office, and disqualification to hold and enjoy any Office of honor, Trust or Profit under the United States: but the Party convicted shall nevertheless be liable and subject to Indictment, Trial, Judgment and Punishment, according to Law.

SECTION 4. The Times, Places and Manner of holding Elections for Senators and Representatives, shall be prescribed in each State by the Legislature thereof; but the Congress may at any time by Law make or alter such Regulations, except as to the Places of chusing Senators.

The Congress shall assemble at least once in every Year, and such Meeting shall be on the first Monday in December, unless they shall by Law appoint a different Day.

SECTION 5. Each House shall be the Judge of the Elections, Returns and Qualifications of its own Members, and a Majority of each shall constitute a Quorum to do Business; but a smaller Number may adjourn from day to day, and may be authorized to compel the Attendance of absent Members, in such Manner, and under such Penalties as each House may provide.

Each House may determine the Rules of its Proceedings, punish its Members for disorderly Behaviour, and, with the Concurrence of two thirds, expel a Member.

Each House shall keep a Journal of its Proceedings, and from time to time publish the same, excepting such Parts as may in their Judgment require Secrecy; and the Yeas and Nays of the Members of either House on any question shall, at the Desire of one fifth of those Present, be entered on the Journal.

Neither House, during the Session of Congress, shall, without the Consent of the other, adjourn for more than three days, nor to any other Place than that in which the two Houses shall be sitting.

SECTION 6. The Senators and Representatives shall receive a Compensation for their Services, to be ascertained by Law, and paid out of the Treasury of the United States. They shall in all Cases, except Treason, Felony and Breach of the Peace, be privileged from Arrest during their Attendance at the Session of their respective Houses, and in going to and returning from the same; and for any Speech or Debate in either House, they shall not be questioned in any other Place.

No Senator or Representative shall, during the Time for which he was elected, be appointed to any civil Office under the Authority of the United States, which shall have been created, or the Emoluments whereof shall have been encreased during such time; and no Person holding any Office under the United States, shall be a Member of either House during his Continuance in Office.

SECTION 7. All Bills for raising Revenue shall originate in the House of Representatives; but the Senate may propose or concur with Amendments as on other Bills.

Every Bill which shall have passed the House of Representatives and the Senate, shall, before it become a Law, be presented to the President of the United States, If he approve he shall sign it, but if not he shall return it, with his Objections to that House in which it shall have originated, who shall enter the Objections at large on their Journal, and proceed to reconsider it. If after such Reconsideration two thirds of that House shall agree to pass the Bill, it shall be sent, together with the Objections, to the other House, by which it shall likewise be reconsidered, and if approved by two thirds of that House, it shall become a Law. But in all such Cases the Votes of both Houses shall be determined by yeas and Nays, and the Names of the Persons voting for and against the Bill shall be entered on the Journal of each House respectively. If any Bill shall not be returned by the President within ten Days (Sundays excepted) after it shall have been presented to him, the Same shall be a Law, in like Manner as if he had signed it, unless the Congress by their Adjournment prevent its Return, in which Case it shall not be a Law.

Every Order, Resolution, or Vote to which the Concurrence of the Senate and House of Representatives may be necessary (except on a question of Adjournment) shall be presented to the President of the United States; and before the Same shall take Effect, shall be approved by him, or being disapproved by him, shall be repassed by two thirds of the Senate and House of Representatives, according to the Rules and Limitations prescribed in the Case of a Bill.

SECTION 8. The Congress shall have Power To lay and collect Taxes, Duties, Imposts and Excises, to pay the Debts and provide for the common Defence and general Welfare of the United States; but all Duties, Imposts and Excises shall be uniform throughout the United States;

To borrow Money on the credit of the United States;

To regulate Commerce with foreign Nations, and among the several States, and with the Indian Tribes;

To establish an uniform Rule of Naturalization, and uniform Laws on the subject of Bankruptcies throughout the United States;

To coin Money, regulate the Value thereof, and of foreign Coin, and fix the Standard of Weights and Measures;

To provide for the Punishment of counterfeiting the Securities and current Coin of the United States;

To establish Post Offices and post Roads;

To promote the Progress of Science and useful Arts, by securing for limited Times to Authors and Inventors the exclusive Right to their respective Writings and Discoveries;

To constitute Tribunals inferior to the supreme Court;

To define and punish Piracies and Felonies committed on the high Seas, and Offences against the Law of Nations;

To declare War, grant Letters of Marque and Reprisal, and make Rules concerning Captures on Land and Water;

To raise and support Armies, but no Appropriation of Money to that Use shall be for a longer Term than two Years;

To provide and maintain a Navy;

To make Rules for the Government and Regulation of the land and naval Forces;

To provide for calling forth the Militia to execute the Laws of the Union, suppress Insurrections and repel Invasions;

To provide for organizing, arming, and disciplining, the Militia, and for governing such Part of them as may be employed in the Service of the United States, reserving to the States respectively, the Appointment of the Officers, and the Authority of training the Militia according to the discipline prescribed by Congress;

To exercise exclusive Legislation in all Cases whatsoever, over such District (not exceeding ten Miles square) as may, by Cession of particular States, and the Acceptance of Congress, become the Seat of the Government of the United States, and to exercise like Authority over all Places purchased by the Consent of the Legislature of the State in which the Same shall be, for the Erection of Forts, Magazines, Arsenals, dock-Yards, and other needful Buildings; — And

To make all Laws which shall be necessary and proper for carrying into Execution the foregoing Powers, and all other Powers vested by this Constitution in the Government of the United States, or in any Department or Officer thereof.

SECTION 9. The Migration or Importation of such Persons as any of the States now existing shall think proper to admit, shall not be prohibited by the Congress prior to the Year one thousand eight hundred and eight, but a Tax or duty may be imposed on such Importation, not exceeding ten dollars for each Person.

The Privilege of the Writ of Habeas Corpus shall not be suspended, unless when in Cases of Rebellion or Invasion the public Safety may require it.

No Bill of Attainder or ex post facto Law shall be passed.

No Capitation, or other direct, Tax shall be laid, unless in Proportion to the Census or Enumeration herein before directed to be taken.

No Tax or Duty shall be laid on Articles exported from any State.

No Preference shall be given by any Regulation of Commerce or Revenue to the Ports of one State over those of another; nor shall Vessels bound to, or from, one State, be obliged to enter, clear, or pay Duties in another.

No Money shall be drawn from the Treasury, but in Consequence of Appropriations made by Law; and a regular Statement and Account of the Receipts and Expenditures of all public Money shall be published from time to time.

No Title of Nobility shall be granted by the United States: And no Person holding any Office of Profit or Trust under them, shall, without the Consent of the Congress, accept of any present, Emolument, Office, or Title, of any kind whatever, from any King, Prince, or foreign State.

SECTION 10. No State shall enter into any Treaty, Alliance, or Confederation; grant Letters of Marque and Reprisal; coin Money; emit Bills of Credit; make any Thing but gold and silver Coin a Tender in Payment of Debts; pass any Bill of Attainder, ex post facto Law, or Law impairing the Obligation of Contracts, or grant any Title of Nobility.

No State shall, without the Consent of the Congress, lay any Imposts or Duties on Imports or Exports, except what may be absolutely necessary for executing it's inspection Laws; and the net Produce of all Duties and Imposts, laid by any State on Imports or Exports, shall be for the Use of the Treasury of the United States; and all such Laws shall be subject to the Revision and Controul of the Congress.

No State shall, without the Consent of Congress, lay any Duty of Tonnage, keep Troops, or Ships of War in time of Peace, enter into any Agreement or Compact with another State, or with a foreign Power, or engage in War, unless actually invaded, or in such imminent Danger as will not admit of delay.

ARTICLE II

SECTION 1. The executive Power shall be vested in a President of the United States of America. He shall hold his Office during the Term of four Years, and, together with the Vice President, chosen for the same Term, be elected, as follows:

Each State shall appoint, in such Manner as the Legislature thereof may direct, a Number of Electors, equal to the whole Number of Senators and Representatives to which the State may be entitled in the Congress: but no Senator or Representative, or Person holding an Office of Trust or Profit under the United States, shall be appointed an Elector.

The Electors shall meet in their respective States, and vote by Ballot for two Persons, of whom one at least shall not be an Inhabitant of the same State with themselves. And they shall make a List of all the Persons voted for, and of the Number of Votes for each; which List they shall sign and certify, and transmit sealed to the Seat of the Government of the United States, directed to the President of the Senate. The President of the Senate shall, in the Presence of the Senate and House of Representatives, open all the Certificates, and the Votes shall then be counted. The Person having the greatest Number of Votes shall be the President, if such Number be a Majority of the whole Number of Electors appointed; and if there be more than one who have such Majority, and have an equal Number of Votes, then the House of Representatives shall immediately chuse by Ballot one of them for President; and if no Person have a Majority, then from the five highest on the List the said House shall in like Manner chuse the President. But in chusing the President, the Votes shall be taken by States, the Representation from each State having one Vote; a quorum for this Purpose shall consist of a Member or Members from two thirds of the States, and a Majority of all the States shall be necessary to a Choice. In every Case, after the Choice of the President, the Person having the greatest Number of Votes of the Electors shall be the Vice President.

But if there should remain two or more who have equal Votes, the Senate shall chuse from them by Ballot the Vice President.

The Congress may determine the Time of chusing the Electors, and the Day on which they shall give their Votes; which Day shall be the same throughout the United States.

No Person except a natural born Citizen, or a Citizen of the United States, at the time of the Adoption of this Constitution, shall be eligible to the Office of President; neither shall any Person be eligible to that Office who shall not have attained to the Age of thirty five Years, and been fourteen Years a Resident within the United States.

In Case of the Removal of the President from Office, or of his Death, Resignation, or Inability to discharge the Powers and Duties of the said Office, the Same shall devolve on the Vice President, and the Congress may by Law provide for the Case of Removal, Death, Resignation or Inability, both of the President and Vice President, declaring what Officer shall then act as President, and such Officer shall act accordingly, until the Disability be removed, or a President shall be elected.

The President shall, at stated Times, receive for his Services, a Compensation, which shall neither be increased nor diminished during the Period for which he shall have been elected, and he shall not receive within that Period any other Emolument from the United States, or any of them.

Before he enter on the Execution of his Office, he shall take the following Oath or Affirmation: — "I do solemnly swear (or affirm) that I will faithfully execute the Office of President of the United States, and will to the best of my Ability, preserve, protect and defend the Constitution of the United States."

SECTION 2. The President shall be Commander in Chief of the Army and Navy of the United States, and of the Militia of the several States, when called into the actual Service of the United States; he may require the Opinion, in writing, of the principal Officer in each of the executive Departments, upon any Subject relating to the Duties of their respective Offices, and he shall have Power to grant Reprieves and Pardons for Offences against the United States, except in Cases of Impeachment.

He shall have Power, by and with the Advice and Consent of the Senate, to make Treaties, provided two thirds of the Senators present concur; and he shall nominate, and by and with the Advice and

Consent of the Senate, shall appoint Ambassadors, other public Ministers and Consuls, Judges of the supreme Court, and all other Officers of the United States, whose Appointments are not herein otherwise provided for, and which shall be established by Law: but the Congress may by Law vest the Appointment of such inferior Officers, as they think proper, in the President alone, in the Courts of Law, or in the Heads of Departments.

The President shall have Power to fill up all Vacancies that may happen during the Recess of the Senate, by granting Commissions which shall expire at the End of their next Session.

SECTION 3. He shall from time to time give to the Congress Information of the State of the Union, and recommend to their Consideration such Measures as he shall judge necessary and expedient; he may, on extraordinary Occasions, convene both Houses, or either of them, and in Case of Disagreement between them, with Respect to the Time of Adjournment, he may adjourn them to such Time as he shall think proper; he shall receive Ambassadors and other public Ministers; he shall take Care that the Laws be faithfully executed, and shall Commission all the Officers of the United States.

SECTION 4. The President, Vice President and all civil Officers of the United States, shall be removed from Office on Impeachment for, and Conviction of, Treason, Bribery, or other high Crimes and Misdemeanors.

ARTICLE III

SECTION 1. The judicial Power of the United States shall be vested in one supreme Court, and in such inferior Courts as the Congress may from time to time ordain and establish. The Judges, both of the supreme and inferior Courts, shall hold their Offices during good Behaviour, and shall, at stated Times, receive for their Services a Compensation, which shall not be diminished during their Continuance in Office.

SECTION 2. The judicial Power shall extend to all Cases, in Law and Equity, arising under this Constitution, the Laws of the United States, and Treaties made, or which shall be made, under their Authority; — to all Cases affecting Ambassadors, other public Ministers and Consuls; — to all Cases of admiralty and maritime Jurisdiction; — to Controversies to which the United States shall be a Party; — to Controversies between two or more States; — between a State and Citizens of another State; — between Citizens of different States; — between Citizens of the same State claiming Lands under Grants of different States, and between a State, or the Citizens thereof, and foreign States, Citizens or Subjects.

In all Cases affecting Ambassadors, other public Ministers and Consuls, and those in which a State shall be Party, the supreme Court shall have original Jurisdiction. In all the other Cases before mentioned, the supreme Court shall have appellate Jurisdiction, both as to Law and Fact, with such Exceptions, and under such Regulations as the Congress shall make.

The Trial of all Crimes, except in Cases of Impeachment, shall be by Jury; and such Trial shall be held in the State where the said Crimes shall have been committed; but when not committed within any State, the Trial shall be at such Place or Places as the Congress may by Law have directed.

SECTION 3. Treason against the United States shall consist only in levying War against them, or in adhering to their Enemies, giving them Aid and Comfort. No Person shall be convicted of Treason unless on the Testimony of two Witnesses to the same overt Act, or on Confession in open Court.

The Congress shall have Power to declare the Punishment of Treason, but no Attainder of Treason shall work Corruption of Blood, or Forfeiture except during the Life of the Person attainted.

ARTICLE IV

SECTION 1. Full Faith and Credit shall be given in each State to the public Acts, Records, and judicial Proceedings of every other State. And the Congress may by general Laws prescribe the Manner in which such Acts, Records and Proceedings shall be proved, and the Effect thereof.

SECTION 2. The Citizens of each State shall be entitled to all Privileges and Immunities of Citizens in the several States.

A Person charged in any State with Treason, Felony, or other Crime, who shall flee from Justice, and be found in another State, shall on Demand of the executive Authority of the State from which he fled, be delivered up, to be removed to the State having Jurisdiction of the Crime.

No Person held to Service or Labour in one State, under the Laws thereof, escaping into another, shall, in Consequence of any Law or Regulation therein, be discharged from such Service or Labour, but shall be delivered up on Claim of the Party to whom such Service or Labour may be due.

SECTION 3. New States may be admitted by the Congress into this Union; but no new State shall be formed or erected within the Jurisdiction of any other State; nor any State be formed by the Junction of two or more States, or Parts of States, without the Consent of the Legislatures of the States concerned as well as of the Congress.

The Congress shall have Power to dispose of and make all needful Rules and Regulations respecting the Territory or other Property belonging to the United States; and nothing in this Constitution shall be so construed as to Prejudice any Claims of the United States, or of any particular State.

SECTION 4. The United States shall guarantee to every State in this Union a Republican Form of Government, and shall protect each of them against Invasion; and on Application of the Legislature, or of the Executive (when the Legislature cannot be convened), against domestic Violence.

ARTICLE V

The Congress, whenever two thirds of both Houses shall deem it necessary, shall propose Amendments to this Constitution, or, on the Application of the Legislatures of two thirds of the several States, shall call a Convention for proposing Amendments, which, in either Case, shall be valid to all Intents and Purposes, as Part of this Constitution, when ratified by the Legislatures of three fourths of the several States, or by Conventions in three fourths thereof, as the one or the other Mode of Ratification may be proposed by the Congress; Provided that no Amendment which may be made prior to the Year One thousand eight hundred and eight shall in any Manner affect the first and fourth Clauses in the Ninth Section of the first Article; and that no State, without its Consent, shall be deprived of its equal Suffrage in the Senate.

ARTICLE VI

All Debts contracted and Engagements entered into, before the Adoption of this Constitution, shall be as valid against the United States under this Constitution, as under the Confederation.

This Constitution, and the Laws of the United States which shall be made in Pursuance thereof; and all Treaties made, or which shall be made, under the Authority of the United States, shall be the supreme Law of the Land; and the Judges in every State shall be bound thereby, any Thing in the Constitution or Laws of any State to the Contrary notwithstanding.

The Senators and Representatives before mentioned, and the Members of the several State Legislatures, and all executive and judicial Officers, both of the United States and of the several States, shall be bound by Oath or Affirmation, to support this Constitution; but no religious Test shall ever be required as a Qualification to any Office or public Trust under the United States.

ARTICLE VII

The Ratification of the Conventions of nine States, shall be sufficient for the Establishment of this Constitution between the States so ratifying the Same.

Done in Convention by the Unanimous Consent of the States present the Seventeenth Day of September in the Year of our Lord one thousand seven hundred and Eighty seven and of the Independence of the United States of America the Twelfth In witness whereof We have hereunto subscribed our Names.

FEDERALIST No. 31: *The Same Subject Continued (Concerning the General Power of Taxation)*

Publication: New York Packet

Date: January 1, 1788

Author: Alexander Hamilton

To the People of the State of New York:

IN DISQUISITIONS of every kind, there are certain primary truths, or first principles, upon which all subsequent reasonings must depend. These contain an internal evidence which, antecedent to all reflection or combination, commands the assent of the mind. Where it produces not this effect, it must proceed either from some defect or disorder in the organs of perception, or from the influence of some strong interest, or passion, or prejudice. Of this nature are the maxims in geometry, that "the whole is greater than its part; things equal to the same are equal to one another; two straight lines cannot enclose a space; and all right angles are equal to each other." Of the same nature are these other maxims in ethics and politics, that there cannot be an effect without a cause; that the means ought to be proportioned to the end; that every power ought to be commensurate with its object; that there ought to be no limitation of a power destined to effect a purpose which is itself incapable of limitation. And there are other truths in the two latter sciences which, if they cannot pretend to rank in the class of axioms, are yet such direct inferences from them, and so obvious in themselves, and so agreeable to the natural and unsophisticated dictates of common-sense, that they challenge the assent of a sound and unbiased mind, with a degree of force and conviction almost equally irresistible.

The objects of geometrical inquiry are so entirely abstracted from those pursuits which stir up and put in motion the unruly passions of the human heart, that mankind, without difficulty, adopt not only the more simple theorems of the science, but even those abstruse paradoxes which, however they may appear susceptible of demonstration, are at variance with the natural conceptions which the mind, without the aid of philosophy, would be led to entertain upon the subject. The INFINITE DIVISIBILITY of matter, or, in other words, the INFINITE divisibility of a FINITE thing, extending even to the minutest atom, is a point agreed among geometricians, though not less incomprehensible to common-sense than any of those mysteries in religion, against which the batteries of infidelity have been so industriously leveled.

But in the sciences of morals and politics, men are found far less tractable. To a certain degree, it is right and useful that this should be the case. Caution and investigation are a necessary armor against error and imposition. But this untractableness may be carried too far, and may degenerate into obstinacy, perverseness, or disingenuity. Though it cannot be pretended that the principles of moral and political knowledge have, in general, the same degree of certainty with those of the mathematics, yet they have much better claims in this respect than, to judge from the conduct of men in particular situations, we should be disposed to allow them. The obscurity is much oftener in the passions and prejudices of the reasoner than in the subject. Men, upon too many occasions, do not give their own understandings fair play; but, yielding to some untoward bias, they entangle themselves in words and confound themselves in subtleties.

How else could it happen (if we admit the objectors to be sincere in their opposition), that positions so clear as those which manifest the necessity of a general power of taxation in the government of the Union, should have to encounter any adversaries among men of discernment? Though these positions have been elsewhere fully stated, they will perhaps not be improperly recapitulated in this place, as introductory to an examination of what may have been offered by way of objection to them. They are in substance as follows:

A government ought to contain in itself every power requisite to the full accomplishment of the objects committed to its care, and to the complete execution of the trusts for which it is responsible, free from every other control but a regard to the public good and to the sense of the people.

As the duties of superintending the national defense and of securing the public peace against foreign or domestic violence involve a provision for casualties and dangers to which no possible limits can be assigned, the power of making that provision ought to know no other bounds than the exigencies of the nation and the resources of the community.

As revenue is the essential engine by which the means of answering the national exigencies must be procured, the power of procuring that article in its full extent must necessarily be comprehended in that of providing for those exigencies.

As theory and practice conspire to prove that the power of procuring revenue is unavailing when exercised over the States in their collective capacities, the federal government must of necessity be invested with an unqualified power of taxation in the ordinary modes.

Did not experience evince the contrary, it would be natural to conclude that the propriety of a general power of taxation in the national government might safely be permitted to rest on the evidence of these propositions, unassisted by any additional arguments or illustrations. But we find, in fact, that the antagonists of the proposed Constitution, so far from acquiescing in their justness or truth, seem to make their principal and most zealous effort against this part of the plan. It may therefore be satisfactory to analyze the arguments with which they combat it.

Those of them which have been most labored with that view, seem in substance to amount to this: "It is not true, because the exigencies of the Union may not be susceptible of limitation, that its power of laying taxes ought to be unconfined. Revenue is as requisite to the purposes of the local administrations as to those of the Union; and the former are at least of equal importance with the latter to the happiness of the people. It is, therefore, as necessary that the State governments should be able to command the means of supplying their wants, as that the national government should possess the like faculty in respect to the wants of the Union. But an indefinite power of taxation in the LATTER might, and probably would in time, deprive the FORMER of the means of providing for their own necessities; and would subject them entirely to the mercy of the national legislature. As the laws of the Union are to become the supreme law of the land, as it is to have power to pass all laws that may be NECESSARY for carrying into execution the authorities with which it is proposed to vest it, the national government might at any time abolish the taxes imposed for State objects upon the pretense of an interference with its own. It might allege a necessity of doing this in order to give efficacy to the national revenues. And thus all the resources of taxation might by degrees become the subjects of federal monopoly, to the entire exclusion and destruction of the State governments."

This mode of reasoning appears sometimes to turn upon the supposition of usurpation in the national government; at other times it seems to be designed only as a deduction from the constitutional operation of its intended powers. It is only in the latter light that it can be admitted to have any pretensions to fairness. The moment we launch into conjectures about the usurpations of the federal government, we get into an unfathomable abyss, and fairly put ourselves out of the reach of all reasoning. Imagination may range at pleasure till it gets bewildered amidst the labyrinths of an enchanted castle, and knows not on which side to turn to extricate itself from the perplexities into which it has so rashly adventured. Whatever may be the limits or modifications of the powers of the Union, it is easy to imagine an endless train of possible dangers; and by indulging an excess of jealousy and timidity, we may bring ourselves to a state of absolute scepticism and irresolution. I repeat here what I have observed in substance in another place, that all observations founded upon the danger of usurpation ought to be referred to the composition and structure of the government, not to the nature or extent of its powers. The State governments, by their original constitutions, are invested with complete sovereignty. In what does our security consist against usurpation from that quarter? Doubtless in the manner of their formation, and in a due dependence of those who are to administer them upon the people. If the proposed construction of the federal government be found, upon an impartial examination of it, to be such as to afford, to a proper extent, the same species of security, all apprehensions on the score of usurpation ought to be discarded.

It should not be forgotten that a disposition in the State governments to encroach upon the rights of the Union is quite as probable as a disposition in the Union to encroach upon the rights of the State governments. What side would be likely to prevail in such a conflict, must depend on the means which the contending parties could employ toward insuring success. As in republics strength is always on the side of the people, and as there are weighty reasons to induce a belief that the State governments will commonly possess most influence over them, the natural conclusion is that such contests will be most apt to end to the disadvantage of the Union; and that there is greater probability of encroachments by the members upon the federal head, than by the federal head upon the members. But it is evident that all conjectures of this kind must be extremely vague and fallible: and that it is by far the safest course to lay them altogether aside, and to confine our attention wholly to the nature and extent of the powers as they are delineated in the Constitution. Every thing beyond this must be left to the prudence and firmness of the people; who, as they will hold the scales in their own hands, it is to be hoped, will always take care to preserve the constitutional equilibrium between the general and the State governments. Upon this ground, which is evidently the true one, it will not be difficult to obviate the objections which have been made to an indefinite power of taxation in the United States.

PUBLIUS

FEDERALIST No. 33: *The Same Subject Continued (Concerning the General Power of Taxation)*

Publication: The Independent Journal

Date: January 2, 1788

Author: Alexander Hamilton

To the People of the State of New York:

THE residue of the argument against the provisions of the Constitution in respect to taxation is ingrafted upon the following clause. The last clause of the eighth section of the first article of the plan under consideration authorizes the national legislature "to make all laws which shall be NECESSARY and PROPER for carrying into execution THE POWERS by that Constitution vested in the government of the United States, or in any department or officer thereof"; and the second clause of the sixth article declares, "that the Constitution and the laws of the United States made IN PURSUANCE THEREOF, and the treaties made by their authority shall be the SUPREME LAW of the land, any thing in the constitution or laws of any State to the contrary notwithstanding."

These two clauses have been the source of much virulent invective and petulant declamation against the proposed Constitution. They have been held up to the people in all the exaggerated colors of misrepresentation as the pernicious engines by which their local governments were to be destroyed and their liberties exterminated; as the hideous monster whose devouring jaws would spare neither sex nor age, nor high nor low, nor sacred nor profane; and yet, strange as it may appear, after all this clamor, to those who may not have happened to contemplate them in the same light, it may be affirmed with perfect confidence that the constitutional operation of the intended government would be precisely the same, if these clauses were entirely obliterated, as if they were repeated in every article. They are only declaratory of a truth which would have resulted by necessary and unavoidable implication from the very act of constituting a federal government, and vesting it with certain specified powers. This is so clear a proposition, that moderation itself can scarcely listen to the railings which have been so copiously vented against this part of the plan, without emotions that disturb its equanimity.

What is a power, but the ability or faculty of doing a thing? What is the ability to do a thing, but the power of employing the MEANS necessary to its execution? What is a LEGISLATIVE power, but a power of making LAWS? What are the MEANS to execute a LEGISLATIVE power but LAWS? What is the power of laying and collecting taxes, but a LEGISLATIVE POWER, or a power of MAKING LAWS, to lay and collect taxes? What are the proper means of executing such a power, but NECESSARY and PROPER laws?

This simple train of inquiry furnishes us at once with a test by which to judge of the true nature of the clause complained of. It conducts us to this palpable truth, that a power to lay and collect taxes must be a power to pass all laws NECESSARY and PROPER for the execution of that power; and what does the unfortunate and calumniated provision in question do more than declare the same truth, to wit, that the national legislature, to whom the power of laying and collecting taxes had been previously given, might, in the execution of that power, pass all laws NECESSARY and PROPER to carry it into effect? I have applied these observations thus particularly to the power of taxation, because it is the immediate subject under consideration, and because it is the most important of the authorities proposed to be conferred upon the Union. But the same process will lead to the same result, in relation to all other powers declared in the Constitution. And it is EXPRESSLY to execute these powers that the sweeping clause, as it has been affectedly called, authorizes the national legislature to pass all NECESSARY and PROPER laws. If there is any thing exceptionable, it must be sought for in the specific powers upon which this general declaration is predicated. The declaration itself, though it may be chargeable with tautology or redundancy, is at least perfectly harmless.

But SUSPICION may ask, Why then was it introduced? The answer is, that it could only have been done for greater caution, and to guard against all cavilling refinements in those who might hereafter feel a disposition to curtail and evade the legitimate authorities of the Union. The Convention probably foresaw, what it has been a principal aim of these papers to inculcate, that the danger which most threatens our political welfare is that the State governments will finally sap the foundations of the Union; and might therefore think it necessary, in so cardinal a point, to leave nothing to construction. Whatever may have been the inducement to it, the wisdom of the precaution is evident from the cry which has been raised against it; as that very cry betrays a disposition to question the great and essential truth which it is manifestly the object of that provision to declare.

But it may be again asked, Who is to judge of the NECESSITY and PROPRIETY of the laws to be passed for executing the powers of the Union? I answer, first, that this question arises as well and as fully upon the simple grant of those powers as upon the declaratory clause; and I answer, in the second place, that the national government, like every other, must judge, in the first instance, of the proper exercise of its powers, and its constituents in the last. If the federal government should overpass the just bounds of its authority and make a tyrannical use of its powers, the people, whose creature it is, must appeal to the standard they have formed, and take such measures to redress the injury done to the Constitution as the exigency may suggest and prudence justify. The propriety of a law, in a constitutional light, must always be determined by the nature of the powers upon which it is founded. Suppose, by some forced constructions of its authority (which, indeed, cannot easily be imagined), the Federal legislature should attempt to vary the law of descent in any State, would it not be evident that, in making such an attempt, it had exceeded its jurisdiction, and infringed upon that of the State? Suppose, again, that upon the pretense of an interference with its revenues, it should undertake to abrogate a landtax imposed by the authority of a State; would it not be equally evident that this was an invasion of that concurrent jurisdiction in respect to this species of tax, which its Constitution plainly supposes to exist in the State governments? If there ever should be a doubt on this head, the credit of it will be entirely due to those reasoners who, in the imprudent zeal of their animosity to the plan of the convention, have labored to envelop it in a cloud calculated to obscure the plainest and simplest truths.

But it is said that the laws of the Union are to be the SUPREME LAW of the land. But what inference can be drawn from this, or what would they amount to, if they were not to be supreme? It is evident they would amount to nothing. A LAW, by the very meaning of the term, includes supremacy. It is a rule which those to whom it is prescribed are bound to observe. This results from every political association. If individuals enter into a state of society, the laws of that society must be the supreme regulator of their conduct. If a number of political societies enter into a larger political society, the laws which the latter may enact, pursuant to the powers intrusted to it by its constitution, must necessarily be supreme over those societies, and the individuals of whom they are composed. It would otherwise be a mere treaty, dependent on the good faith of the parties, and not a government, which is only another word for POLITICAL POWER AND SUPREMACY. But it will not follow from this doctrine that acts of the large society which are NOT PURSUANT to its constitutional powers, but which are invasions of the residuary authorities of the smaller societies, will become the supreme law of the land. These will be merely acts of usurpation, and will deserve to be treated as such. Hence we perceive that the clause which declares the supremacy of the laws of the Union, like the one we have just before considered, only declares a truth, which flows immediately and necessarily from the institution of a federal government. It will not, I presume, have escaped observation, that it EXPRESSLY confines this supremacy to laws made PURSUANT TO THE CONSTITUTION; which I mention merely as an instance of caution in the convention; since that limitation would have been to be understood, though it had not been expressed.

Though a law, therefore, laying a tax for the use of the United States would be supreme in its nature, and could not legally be opposed or controlled, yet a law for abrogating or preventing the collection of a tax laid by the authority of the State, (unless upon imports and exports), would not be the supreme law of the land, but a usurpation of power not granted by the Constitution. As far as an improper accumulation of taxes on the same object might tend to render the collection difficult or precarious, this would be a mutual inconvenience, not arising from a superiority or defect of power on either side, but from an injudicious exercise of power by one or the other, in a manner equally disadvantageous to both. It is to be hoped and presumed, however, that mutual interest would dictate a concert in this respect which would avoid any material inconvenience. The inference from the whole is, that the individual States would, under the proposed Constitution, retain an independent and uncontrollable authority to raise revenue to any extent of which they may stand in need, by every kind of taxation, except duties on imports and exports. It will be shown in the next paper that this CONCURRENT JURISDICTION in the article of taxation was the only admissible substitute for an entire subordination, in respect to this branch of power, of the State authority to that of the Union.

PUBLIUS

FEDERALIST No. 34: *The Same Subject Continued (Concerning the General Power of Taxation)*

Publication: The Independent Journal

Date: January 5, 1788

Author: Alexander Hamilton

To the People of the State of New York:

I FLATTER myself it has been clearly shown in my last number that the particular States, under the proposed Constitution, would have COEQUAL authority with the Union in the article of revenue, except as to duties on imports. As this leaves open to the States far the greatest part of the resources of the community, there can be no color for the assertion that they would not possess means as abundant as could be desired for the supply of their own wants, independent of all external control. That the field is sufficiently wide will more fully appear when we come to advert to the inconsiderable share of the public expenses for which it will fall to the lot of the State governments to provide.

To argue upon abstract principles that this co-ordinate authority cannot exist, is to set up supposition and theory against fact and reality. However proper such reasonings might be to show that a thing OUGHT NOT TO EXIST, they are wholly to be rejected when they are made use of to prove that it does not exist contrary to the evidence of the fact itself. It is well known that in the Roman republic the legislative authority, in the last resort, resided for ages in two different political bodies not as branches of the same legislature, but as distinct and independent legislatures, in each of which an opposite interest prevailed: in one the patrician; in the other, the plebian. Many arguments might have been adduced to prove the unfitness of two such seemingly contradictory authorities, each having power to ANNUL or REPEAL the acts of the other. But a man would have been regarded as frantic who should have attempted at Rome to disprove their existence. It will be readily understood that I allude to the COMITIA CENTURIATA and the COMITIA TRIBUTA. The former, in which the people voted by centuries, was so arranged as to give a superiority to the patrician interest; in the latter, in which numbers prevailed, the plebian interest had an entire predominancy. And yet these two legislatures coexisted for ages, and the Roman republic attained to the utmost height of human greatness.

In the case particularly under consideration, there is no such contradiction as appears in the example cited; there is no power on either side to annul the acts of the other. And in practice there is little reason to apprehend any inconvenience; because, in a short course of time, the wants of the States will naturally reduce themselves within A VERY NARROW COMPASS; and in the interim, the United States will, in all probability, find it convenient to abstain wholly from those objects to which the particular States would be inclined to resort.

To form a more precise judgment of the true merits of this question, it will be well to advert to the proportion between the objects that will require a federal provision in respect to revenue, and those which will require a State provision. We shall discover that the former are altogether unlimited, and that the latter are circumscribed within very moderate bounds. In pursuing this inquiry, we must bear in mind that we are not to confine our view to the present period, but to look forward to remote futurity. Constitutions of civil government are not to be framed upon a calculation of existing exigencies, but upon a combination of these with the probable exigencies of ages, according to the natural and tried course of human affairs. Nothing, therefore, can be more fallacious than to infer the extent of any power, proper to be lodged in the national government, from an estimate of its immediate necessities. There ought to be a CAPACITY to provide for future contingencies as they may happen; and as these are illimitable in their nature, it is impossible safely to limit that capacity. It is true, perhaps, that a computation might be made with sufficient accuracy to answer the purpose of the quantity of revenue requisite to discharge the subsisting engagements of the Union, and to maintain those establishments which, for some time to come, would suffice in time of peace. But would it be wise, or would it not rather be the extreme of folly, to stop at this point, and to leave the government intrusted with the care of the national defense in a state of absolute incapacity to provide for the protection of the community against future invasions of the public peace, by foreign war or domestic convulsions? If, on the contrary, we ought to exceed this point, where can we stop, short of an indefinite power of providing for emergencies as they may arise? Though it is easy to assert, in general terms, the possibility of forming a rational judgment of a due provision against probable dangers, yet we may safely challenge those who make the assertion to bring forward their data, and may affirm that they would be found as vague and uncertain as any that could be produced to establish the probable duration of the world. Observations confined to the mere prospects of internal attacks can deserve no weight; though even these will admit of no satisfactory calculation: but if we mean to be a commercial people, it must form a part of our policy to be able one day to defend that commerce. The support of a navy and of naval wars would involve contingencies that must baffle all the efforts of political arithmetic.

Admitting that we ought to try the novel and absurd experiment in politics of tying up the hands of government from offensive war founded upon reasons of state, yet certainly we ought not to disable it from guarding the community against the ambition or enmity of other nations. A cloud has been for some time hanging over the European world. If it should break forth into a storm, who can insure us that in its progress a part of its fury would not be spent upon us? No reasonable man would hastily pronounce that we are entirely out of its reach. Or if the combustible materials that now seem to be collecting should be dissipated without coming to maturity, or if a flame should be kindled without extending to us, what security can we have that our tranquillity will long remain undisturbed from some other cause or from some other quarter? Let us recollect that peace or war will not always be left to our option; that however moderate or unambitious we may be, we cannot count upon the moderation, or hope to extinguish the ambition of others. Who could have imagined at the conclusion of the last war that France and Britain, wearied and exhausted as they both were, would so soon have looked with so hostile an aspect upon each other? To judge from the history of mankind, we shall be compelled to conclude that the fiery and destructive passions of war reign in the human breast with much more powerful sway than the mild and beneficent sentiments of peace; and that to model our political systems upon speculations of lasting tranquillity, is to calculate on the weaker springs of the human character.

What are the chief sources of expense in every government? What has occasioned that enormous accumulation of debts with which several of the European nations are oppressed? The answers plainly is, wars and rebellions; the support of those institutions which are necessary to guard the body politic against these two most mortal diseases of society. The expenses arising from those institutions which are relative to the mere domestic police of a state, to the support of its legislative, executive, and judicial departments, with their different appendages, and to the encouragement of agriculture and manufactures (which will comprehend almost all the objects of state expenditure), are insignificant in comparison with those which relate to the national defense.

In the kingdom of Great Britain, where all the ostentatious apparatus of monarchy is to be provided for, not above a fifteenth part of the annual income of the nation is appropriated to the class of expenses last mentioned; the other fourteen fifteenths are absorbed in the payment of the interest of debts contracted for carrying on the wars in which that country has been engaged, and in the maintenance of fleets and armies. If, on the one hand, it should be observed that the expenses incurred in the prosecution of the ambitious enterprises and vainglorious pursuits of a monarchy are not a proper standard by which to judge of those which might be necessary in a republic, it ought, on the other hand, to be remarked that there should be as great a disproportion between the profusion and extravagance of a wealthy kingdom in its domestic administration, and the frugality and economy which in that particular become the modest simplicity of republican government. If we balance a proper deduction from one side against that which it is supposed ought to be made from the other, the proportion may still be considered as holding good.

But let us advert to the large debt which we have ourselves contracted in a single war, and let us only calculate on a common share of the events which disturb the peace of nations, and we shall instantly perceive, without the aid of any elaborate illustration, that there must always be an immense disproportion between the objects of federal and state expenditures. It is true that several of the States, separately, are encumbered with considerable debts, which are an excrescence of the late war. But this cannot happen again, if the proposed system be adopted; and when these debts are discharged, the only call for revenue of any consequence, which the State governments will continue to experience, will be for the mere support of their respective civil list; to which, if we add all contingencies, the total amount in every State ought to fall considerably short of two hundred thousand pounds.

In framing a government for posterity as well as ourselves, we ought, in those provisions which are designed to be permanent, to calculate, not on temporary, but on permanent causes of expense. If this principle be a just one our attention would be directed to a provision in favor of the State governments for an annual sum of about two hundred thousand pounds; while the exigencies of the Union could be susceptible of no limits, even in imagination. In this view of the subject, by what logic can it be maintained that the local governments ought to command, in perpetuity, an EXCLUSIVE source of revenue for any sum beyond the extent of two hundred thousand pounds? To extend its power further, in EXCLUSION of the authority of the

Union, would be to take the resources of the community out of those hands which stood in need of them for the public welfare, in order to put them into other hands which could have no just or proper occasion for them.

Suppose, then, the convention had been inclined to proceed upon the principle of a repartition of the objects of revenue, between the Union and its members, in PROPORTION to their comparative necessities; what particular fund could have been selected for the use of the States, that would not either have been too much or too little too little for their present, too much for their future wants? As to the line of separation between external and internal taxes, this would leave to the States, at a rough computation, the command of two thirds of the resources of the community to defray from a tenth to a twentieth part of its expenses; and to the Union, one third of the resources of the community, to defray from nine tenths to nineteen twentieths of its expenses. If we desert this boundary and content ourselves with leaving to the States an exclusive power of taxing houses and lands, there would still be a great disproportion between the MEANS and the END; the possession of one third of the resources of the community to supply, at most, one tenth of its wants. If any fund could have been selected and appropriated, equal to and not greater than the object, it would have been inadequate to the discharge of the existing debts of the particular States, and would have left them dependent on the Union for a provision for this purpose.

The preceding train of observation will justify the position which has been elsewhere laid down, that "A CONCURRENT JURISDICTION in the article of taxation was the only admissible substitute for an entire subordination, in respect to this branch of power, of State authority to that of the Union." Any separation of the objects of revenue that could have been fallen upon, would have amounted to a sacrifice of the great INTERESTS of the Union to the POWER of the individual States. The convention thought the concurrent jurisdiction preferable to that subordination; and it is evident that it has at least the merit of reconciling an indefinite constitutional power of taxation in the Federal government with an adequate and independent power in the States to provide for their own necessities. There remain a few other lights, in which this important subject of taxation will claim a further consideration.

PUBLIUS

FEDERALIST No. 44: *Restrictions on the Authority of the Several States*

Publication: New York Packet

Date: January 25, 1788

Author: James Madison

To the People of the State of New York:

A FIFTH class of provisions in favor of the federal authority consists of the following restrictions on the authority of the several States:

1. "No State shall enter into any treaty, alliance, or confederation; grant letters of marque and reprisal; coin money; emit bills of credit; make any thing but gold and silver a legal tender in payment of debts; pass any bill of attainder, ex post facto law, or law impairing the obligation of contracts; or grant any title of nobility."

The prohibition against treaties, alliances, and confederations makes a part of the existing articles of Union; and for reasons which need no explanation, is copied into the new Constitution. The prohibition of letters of marque is another part of the old system, but is somewhat extended in the new. According to the former, letters of marque could be granted by the States after a declaration of war; according to the latter, these licenses must be obtained, as well during war as previous to its declaration, from the government of the United States. This alteration is fully justified by the advantage of uniformity in all points which relate to foreign powers; and of immediate responsibility to the nation in all those for whose conduct the nation itself is to be responsible.

The right of coining money, which is here taken from the States, was left in their hands by the Confederation, as a concurrent right with that of Congress, under an exception in favor of the exclusive right of Congress to regulate the alloy and value. In this instance, also, the new provision is an improvement on the old. Whilst the alloy and value depended on the general authority, a right of coinage in the particular States could have no other effect than to multiply expensive mints and diversify the forms and weights of the circulating pieces. The latter inconveniency defeats one purpose for which the power was originally submitted to the federal head; and as far as the former might prevent an inconvenient remittance of gold and silver to the central mint for recoinage, the end can be as well attained by local mints established under the general authority.

The extension of the prohibition to bills of credit must give pleasure to every citizen, in proportion to his love of justice and his knowledge of the true springs of public prosperity. The loss which America has sustained since the peace, from the pestilent effects of paper money on the necessary confidence between man and man, on the necessary confidence in the public councils, on the industry and morals of the people, and on the character of republican government, constitutes an enormous debt against the States chargeable with this unadvised measure, which must long remain unsatisfied; or rather an accumulation of guilt, which can be expiated no otherwise than by a voluntary sacrifice on the altar of justice, of the power which has been the instrument of it. In addition to these persuasive considerations, it may be observed, that the same reasons which show the necessity of denying to the States the power of regulating coin, prove with equal force that they ought not to be at liberty to substitute a paper medium in the place of coin. Had every State a right to regulate the value of its coin, there might be as many different currencies as States, and thus the intercourse among them would be impeded; retrospective alterations in its value might be made, and thus the citizens of other States be injured, and animosities be kindled among the States themselves. The subjects of foreign powers might suffer from the same cause, and hence the Union be discredited and embroiled by the indiscretion of a single member. No one of these mischiefs is less incident to a power in the States to emit paper money, than to coin gold or silver. The power to make any thing but gold and silver a tender in payment of debts, is withdrawn from the States, on the same principle with that of issuing a paper currency.

Bills of attainder, ex post facto laws, and laws impairing the obligation of contracts, are contrary to the first principles of the social compact, and to every principle of sound legislation. The two former are expressly prohibited by the declarations prefixed to some of the State constitutions, and all of them are prohibited by the spirit and scope of these fundamental charters. Our own experience has taught us, nevertheless, that additional fences against these dangers ought not to be omitted. Very properly, therefore, have the convention added this constitutional bulwark in favor of personal security and private rights; and I am much deceived if they have not, in so doing, as faithfully consulted the genuine sentiments as the undoubted interests of their constituents. The sober people of America are weary of the fluctuating policy which has directed the public councils. They have seen with regret and indignation that sudden changes and legislative interferences, in cases affecting personal rights, become jobs in the hands of enterprising and influential speculators, and snares to the more-industrious and less-informed part of the community. They have seen, too, that one legislative interference is but the first link of a long chain of repetitions, every subsequent interference being naturally produced by the effects of the preceding. They very rightly infer, therefore, that some thorough reform is wanting, which will banish speculations on public measures, inspire a general prudence and industry, and give a regular course to the business of society. The prohibition with respect to titles of nobility is copied from the articles of Confederation and needs no comment.

2. "No State shall, without the consent of the Congress, lay any imposts or duties on imports or exports, except what may be absolutely necessary for executing its inspection laws, and the net produce of all duties and imposts laid by any State on imports or exports, shall be for the use of the treasury of the United States; and all such laws shall be subject to the revision and control of the Congress. No State shall, without the consent of Congress, lay any duty on tonnage, keep troops or ships of war in time of peace, enter into any agreement or compact with another State, or with a foreign power, or engage in war unless actually invaded, or in such imminent danger as will not admit of delay."

The restraint on the power of the States over imports and exports is enforced by all the arguments which prove the necessity of submitting the regulation of trade to the federal councils. It is needless, therefore, to remark further on this head, than that the manner in which the restraint is qualified seems well calculated at once to secure to the States a reasonable discretion in providing for the conveniency of their imports and exports, and to the United States a reasonable check against the abuse of this discretion. The remaining particulars of this clause fall within reasonings which are either so obvious, or have been so fully developed, that they may be passed over without remark.

The SIXTH and last class consists of the several powers and provisions by which efficacy is given to all the rest.

1. Of these the first is, the "power to make all laws which shall be necessary and proper for carrying into execution the foregoing powers, and all other powers vested by this Constitution in the government of the United States, or in any department or officer thereof."

Few parts of the Constitution have been assailed with more intemperance than this; yet on a fair investigation of it, no part can appear more completely invulnerable. Without the SUBSTANCE of this power, the whole Constitution would be a dead letter. Those who object to the article, therefore, as a part of the Constitution, can only mean that the FORM of the provision is improper. But have they considered whether a better form could have been substituted?

There are four other possible methods which the Constitution might have taken on this subject. They might have copied the second article of the existing Confederation, which would have prohibited the exercise of any power not EXPRESSLY delegated; they might have attempted a positive enumeration of the powers comprehended under the general terms "necessary and proper"; they might have attempted a negative enumeration of them, by specifying the powers excepted from the general definition; they might have been altogether silent on the subject, leaving these necessary and proper powers to construction and inference.

Had the convention taken the first method of adopting the second article of Confederation, it is evident that the new Congress would be continually exposed, as their predecessors have been, to the alternative of construing the term "EXPRESSLY" with so much rigor, as to disarm the government of all real authority whatever, or with so much latitude as to destroy altogether the force of the restriction. It would be easy to show, if it were necessary, that no important power, delegated by the articles of Confederation, has been or can be executed by Congress, without recurring more or less to the doctrine of CONSTRUCTION or IMPLICATION. As the powers delegated under the new system are more extensive, the government which is to administer it would find itself still more distressed with the alternative of betraying the public interests by doing nothing, or of violating the Constitution by exercising powers indispensably necessary and proper, but, at the same time, not EXPRESSLY granted.

Had the convention attempted a positive enumeration of the powers necessary and proper for carrying their other powers into effect, the attempt would have involved a complete digest of laws on every subject to which the Constitution relates; accommodated too, not only to the existing state of things, but to all the possible changes which futurity may produce; for in every new application of a general power, the PARTICULAR POWERS, which are the means of attaining the OBJECT of the general power, must always necessarily vary with that object, and be often properly varied whilst the object remains the same.

Had they attempted to enumerate the particular powers or means not necessary or proper for carrying the general powers into execution, the task would have been no less chimerical; and would have been liable to this further objection, that every defect in the enumeration would have been equivalent to a positive grant of authority. If, to avoid this consequence, they had attempted a partial enumeration of the exceptions, and described the residue by the general terms, NOT NECESSARY OR PROPER, it must have happened that the enumeration would comprehend a few of the excepted powers only; that these would be such as would be least likely to be assumed or tolerated, because the enumeration would of course select such as would be least necessary or proper; and that the unnecessary and improper powers included in the residuum, would be less forcibly excepted, than if no partial enumeration had been made.

Had the Constitution been silent on this head, there can be no doubt that all the particular powers requisite as means of executing the general powers would have resulted to the government, by unavoidable implication. No axiom is more clearly established in law, or in reason, than that wherever the end is required, the means are authorized; wherever a general power to do a thing is given, every particular power necessary for doing it is included. Had this last method, therefore, been pursued by the convention, every objection now urged against their plan would remain in all its plausibility; and the real inconveniency would be incurred of not removing a pretext which may be seized on critical occasions for drawing into question the essential powers of the Union.

If it be asked what is to be the consequence, in case the Congress shall misconstrue this part of the Constitution, and exercise powers not warranted by its true meaning, I answer, the same as if they should misconstrue or enlarge any other power vested in them; as if the general power had been reduced to particulars, and any one of these were to be violated; the same, in short, as if the State legislatures should violate the irrespective constitutional authorities. In the first instance, the success of the usurpation will depend on the executive and judiciary departments, which are to expound and give effect to the legislative acts; and in the last resort a remedy must be obtained from the people who can, by the election of more faithful representatives, annul the acts of the usurpers. The truth is, that this ultimate redress may be more confided in against unconstitutional acts of the federal than of the State legislatures, for this plain reason, that as every such act of the former will be an invasion of the rights of the latter, these will be ever ready to mark the innovation, to sound the alarm to the people, and to exert their local influence in effecting a change of federal representatives. There being no such intermediate body between the State legislatures and the people interested in watching the conduct of the former, violations of the State constitutions are more likely to remain unnoticed and unredressed.

2. "This Constitution and the laws of the United States which shall be made in pursuance thereof, and all treaties made, or which shall be made, under the authority of the United States, shall be the supreme law of the land, and the judges in every State shall be bound thereby, any thing in the constitution or laws of any State to the contrary notwithstanding."

The indiscreet zeal of the adversaries to the Constitution has betrayed them into an attack on this part of it also, without which it would have been evidently and radically defective. To be fully sensible of this, we need only suppose for a moment that the supremacy of the State constitutions had been left complete by a saving clause in their favor.

In the first place, as these constitutions invest the State legislatures with absolute sovereignty, in all cases not excepted by the existing articles of Confederation, all the authorities contained in the proposed Constitution, so far as they exceed those enumerated in the Confederation, would have been annulled, and the new Congress would have been reduced to the same impotent condition with their predecessors.

In the next place, as the constitutions of some of the States do not even expressly and fully recognize the existing powers of the Confederacy, an express saving of the supremacy of the former would, in such States, have brought into question every power contained in the proposed Constitution.

In the third place, as the constitutions of the States differ much from each other, it might happen that a treaty or national law, of great and equal importance to the States, would interfere with some and not with other constitutions, and would consequently be valid in some of the States, at the same time that it would have no effect in others.

In fine, the world would have seen, for the first time, a system of government founded on an inversion of the fundamental principles of all government; it would have seen the authority of the whole society every where subordinate to the authority of the parts; it would have seen a monster, in which the head was under the direction of the members.

3. "The Senators and Representatives, and the members of the several State legislatures, and all executive and judicial officers, both of the

United States and the several States, shall be bound by oath or affirmation to support this Constitution."

It has been asked why it was thought necessary, that the State magistracy should be bound to support the federal Constitution, and unnecessary that a like oath should be imposed on the officers of the United States, in favor of the State constitutions.

Several reasons might be assigned for the distinction. I content myself with one, which is obvious and conclusive. The members of the federal government will have no agency in carrying the State constitutions into effect. The members and officers of the State governments, on the contrary, will have an essential agency in giving effect to the federal Constitution. The election of the President and Senate will depend, in all cases, on the legislatures of the several States. And the election of the House of Representatives will equally depend on the same authority in the first instance; and will, probably, forever be conducted by the officers, and according to the laws, of the States.

4. Among the provisions for giving efficacy to the federal powers might be added those which belong to the executive and judiciary departments: but as these are reserved for particular examination in another place, I pass them over in this.

We have now reviewed, in detail, all the articles composing the sum or quantity of power delegated by the proposed Constitution to the federal government, and are brought to this undeniable conclusion, that no part of the power is unnecessary or improper for accomplishing the necessary objects of the Union. The question, therefore, whether this amount of power shall be granted or not, resolves itself into another question, whether or not a government commensurate to the exigencies of the Union shall be established; or, in other words, whether the Union itself shall be preserved.

PUBLIUS

FEDERALIST No. 45: *The Alleged Danger From the Powers of the Union to the State Governments.*

Publication: Independent Journal

Date: January 26, 1788

Author: James Madison

To the People of the State of New York:

HAVING shown that no one of the powers transferred to the federal government is unnecessary or improper, the next question to be considered is, whether the whole mass of them will be dangerous to the portion of authority left in the several States.

The adversaries to the plan of the convention, instead of considering in the first place what degree of power was absolutely necessary for the purposes of the federal government, have exhausted themselves in a secondary inquiry into the possible consequences of the proposed degree of power to the governments of the particular States. But if the Union, as has been shown, be essential to the security of the people of America against foreign danger; if it be essential to their security against contentions and wars among the different States; if it be essential to guard them against those violent and oppressive factions which embitter the blessings of liberty, and against those military establishments which must gradually poison its very fountain; if, in a word, the Union be essential to the happiness of the people of America, is it not preposterous, to urge as an objection to a government, without which the objects of the Union cannot be attained, that such a government may derogate from the importance of the governments of the individual States? Was, then, the American Revolution effected, was the American Confederacy formed, was the precious blood of thousands spilt, and the hard-earned substance of millions lavished, not that the people of America should enjoy peace, liberty, and safety, but that the government of the individual States, that particular municipal establishments, might enjoy a certain extent of power, and be arrayed with certain dignities and attributes of sovereignty? We have heard of the impious doctrine in the Old World, that the people were made for kings, not kings for the people. Is the same doctrine to be revived in the New, in another shape that the solid happiness of the people is to be sacrificed to the views of political institutions of a different form? It is too early for politicians to presume on our forgetting that the public good, the real welfare of the great body of the people, is the supreme object to be pursued; and that no form of government whatever has any other value than as it may be fitted for the attainment of this object. Were the plan of the convention adverse to the public happiness, my voice would be, Reject the plan. Were the Union itself inconsistent with the public happiness, it would be, Abolish the Union. In like manner, as far as the sovereignty of the States cannot be reconciled to the happiness of the people, the voice of every good citizen must be, Let the former be sacrificed to the latter. How far the sacrifice is necessary, has been shown. How far the unsacrificed residue will be endangered, is the question before us.

Several important considerations have been touched in the course of these papers, which discountenance the supposition that the operation of the federal government will by degrees prove fatal to the State governments. The more I revolve the subject, the more fully I am persuaded that the balance is much more likely to be disturbed by the preponderancy of the last than of the first scale.

We have seen, in all the examples of ancient and modern confederacies, the strongest tendency continually betraying itself in the members, to despoil the general government of its authorities, with a very ineffectual capacity in the latter to defend itself against the encroachments. Although, in most of these examples, the system has been so dissimilar from that under consideration as greatly to weaken any inference concerning the latter from the fate of the former, yet, as the States will retain, under the proposed Constitution, a very extensive portion of active sovereignty, the inference ought not to be wholly disregarded. In the Achaean league it is probable that the federal head had a degree and species of power, which gave it a considerable likeness to the government framed by the convention. The Lycian Confederacy, as far as its principles and form are transmitted, must have borne a still greater analogy to it. Yet history does not inform us that either of them ever degenerated, or tended to degenerate, into one consolidated government. On the contrary, we know that the ruin of one of them proceeded from the incapacity of the federal authority to prevent the dissensions, and finally the disunion, of the subordinate authorities. These cases are the more worthy of our attention, as the external causes by which the component parts were pressed together were much more numerous and powerful than in our case; and consequently less powerful ligaments within would be sufficient to bind the members to the head, and to each other.

In the feudal system, we have seen a similar propensity exemplified. Notwithstanding the want of proper sympathy in every instance between the local sovereigns and the people, and the sympathy in some instances between the general sovereign and the latter, it usually happened that the local sovereigns prevailed in the rivalship for encroachments. Had no external dangers enforced internal harmony and subordination, and particularly, had the local sovereigns possessed the affections of the people, the great kingdoms in Europe would at this time consist of as many independent princes as there were formerly feudatory barons.

The State governments will have the advantage of the Federal government, whether we compare them in respect to the immediate dependence of the one on the other; to the weight of personal influence which each side will possess; to the powers respectively vested in them; to the predilection and probable support of the people; to the disposition and faculty of resisting and frustrating the measures of each other.

The State governments may be regarded as constituent and essential parts of the federal government; whilst the latter is nowise essential to the operation or organization of the former. Without the intervention of the State legislatures, the President of the United States cannot be elected at all. They must in all cases have a great share in his appointment, and will, perhaps, in most cases, of themselves determine it. The Senate will be elected absolutely and exclusively by the State legislatures. Even the House of Representatives, though drawn immediately from the people, will be chosen very much under the influence of that class of men, whose influence over the people obtains for themselves an election into the State legislatures. Thus, each of the principal branches of the federal government will owe its existence more or less to the favor of the State governments, and must consequently feel a dependence, which is much more likely to beget a disposition too obsequious than too overbearing towards them. On the other side, the component parts of the State governments will in no instance be indebted for their appointment to the direct agency of the federal government, and very little, if at all, to the local influence of its members.

The number of individuals employed under the Constitution of the United States will be much smaller than the number employed under the particular States. There will consequently be less of personal influence on the side of the former than of the latter. The members of the legislative, executive, and judiciary departments of thirteen and more States, the justices of peace, officers of militia, ministerial officers of justice, with all the county, corporation, and town officers, for three millions and more of people, intermixed, and having particular acquaintance with every class and circle of people, must exceed, beyond all proportion, both in number and influence, those of every description who will be employed in the administration of the federal system. Compare the members of the three great departments of the thirteen States, excluding from the judiciary department the justices of peace, with the members of the corresponding departments of the single government of the Union; compare the militia officers of three millions of people with the military and marine officers of any establishment which is within the compass of probability, or, I may add, of possibility, and in this view alone, we may pronounce the advantage of the States to be decisive. If the federal government is to have collectors of revenue, the State governments will have theirs also. And as those of the former will be principally on the seacoast, and not very numerous, whilst those of the latter will be spread over the face of the country, and will be very numerous, the advantage in this view also lies on the same side. It is true, that the Confederacy is to possess, and may exercise, the power of collecting internal as well as external taxes throughout the States; but it is probable that this power will not be resorted to, except for supplemental purposes of revenue; that an option will then be given to the States to supply their quotas by previous collections of their own; and that the eventual collection, under the immediate authority of the Union, will generally be made by the officers, and according to the rules, appointed by the several States. Indeed it is extremely probable, that in other instances, particularly in the organization of the judicial power, the officers of the States will be clothed with the correspondent authority of the Union. Should it happen, however, that separate collectors of internal revenue should be appointed under the federal government, the influence of the whole number would not bear a comparison with that of the multitude of State officers in the opposite scale. Within every district to which a federal collector would be allotted, there would not be less than thirty or forty, or even more, officers of different descriptions, and many of them persons of character and weight, whose influence would lie on the side of the State.

The powers delegated by the proposed Constitution to the federal government, are few and defined. Those which are to remain in the State governments are numerous and indefinite. The former will be exercised principally on external objects, as war, peace, negotiation, and foreign commerce; with which last the power of taxation will, for the most part, be connected. The powers reserved to the several States will extend to all the objects which, in the ordinary course of affairs, concern the lives, liberties, and properties of the people, and the internal order, improvement, and prosperity of the State.

The operations of the federal government will be most extensive and important in times of war and danger; those of the State governments, in times of peace and security. As the former periods will probably bear a small proportion to the latter, the State governments will here enjoy another advantage over the federal government. The more adequate, indeed, the federal powers may be rendered to the national defense, the less frequent will be those scenes of danger which might favor their ascendancy over the governments of the particular States.

If the new Constitution be examined with accuracy and candor, it will be found that the change which it proposes consists much less in the addition of NEW POWERS to the Union, than in the invigoration of its ORIGINAL POWERS. The regulation of commerce, it is true, is a new power; but that seems to be an addition which few oppose, and from which no apprehensions are entertained. The powers relating to war and peace, armies and fleets, treaties and finance, with the other more considerable powers, are all vested in the existing Congress by the articles of Confederation. The proposed change does not enlarge these powers; it only substitutes a more effectual mode of administering them. The change relating to taxation may be regarded as the most important; and yet the present Congress have as complete authority to REQUIRE of the States indefinite supplies of money for the common defense and general welfare, as the future Congress will have to require them of individual citizens; and the latter will be no more bound than the States themselves have been, to pay the quotas respectively taxed on them. Had the States complied punctually with the articles of Confederation, or could their compliance have been enforced by as peaceable means as may be used with success towards single persons, our past experience is very far from countenancing an opinion, that the State governments would have lost their constitutional powers, and have gradually undergone an entire consolidation. To maintain that such an event would have ensued, would be to say at once, that the existence of the State governments is incompatible with any system whatever that accomplishes the essential purposes of the Union.

PUBLIUS

Essays of an Old Whig: *Essay II*

Publication: Independent Gazetteer

Date: October 17, 1787

Author: Unknown

Mr. PRINTER, Since writing my last, in which I stated some doubts respecting the new federal constitution and expressed a wish that those doubts might be removed, I have met with the printed speech of JAMES WILSON, Esquire.—This speech I find was made for the express purpose of removing objections from the minds of those who doubted, like myself, and wished to be satisfied; and except one or two hard names that have escaped the speaker, it bears the marks of more candor than is to be found in most of the production[s], which have been ushered into the world in support of the same measure. This speech also deserves the more attention as coming from a man of abilities fresh from "THE IMPRESSIONS OF FOUR MONTHS CONSTANT ATTENTION TO THE SUBJECT." The subject however is one of those which it imports us all very carefully to examine. I have therefore paid very considerable attention to his arguments, at the same time that I have examined with some care the foundation upon which they are built. Still I remain unsatisfied; and the more unsatisfied, as I have been disappointed in my hope of conviction, from a quarter, from which so much was to be expected— You will give me leave therefore to state shortly in your paper, some of those difficulties which still remain with me.

The first principle which the gentleman endeavours to establish in his speech is a very important one, if true; and lays a sure foundation to reason upon, in answer to the objection which is made to the new constitution, from the want of a bill of rights. The principle is this: that "in DELEGATING FEDERAL POWERS, the congressional authority is to be collected, NOT FROM TACIT IMPLICATION, but from THE POSITIVE GRANT expressed in the instrument of union," "THAT EVERY THING WHICH IS NOT GIVEN IS RESERVED." If this be a just representation of the matter, the authority of the several states will be sufficient to protect our liberties from the encroachments of Congress, without any continental bill of rights; UNLESS the powers which are EXPRESSLY GIVEN to Congress are TOO LARGE.

Without examining particularly at present, whether the powers EXPRESSLY given to Congress are too large or too small, I shall beg leave to consider, whether the author of this speech is sufficiently accurate in his statement of the proposition above referred to.—To strip it of unnecessary words, the position may be reduced to this short sentence, "that every thing which is not EXPRESSLY given to Congress is reserved;" or in other words "that Congress cannot exercise any power or authority that is not in express words delegated to them."—This certainly is the case under the first articles of confederation which hitherto have been the rule and standard of the powers of Congress; for in the second of those articles "each state retains its sovereignty freedom and independence and every power, jurisdiction and right which is not by this confederation EXPRESSLY delegated to the United States in Congress assembled." It was the misfortune of these articles of confederation that they did not by express words give to Congress power sufficient for the purposes of the union; for Congress could not go beyond those powers so expressly given. The position of the speech, therefore is strictly true if applied to the first articles of confederation; "that every thing which is not expressly given is reserved." We are not however to suppose that the speaker meant insidiously to argue from an article in the old confederation in favor of the new constitution, unless the same thing was also in the new constitution. Let us then fairly examine whether in the proposed new constitution there be any thing from which the gentleman can be justified in his opinion, "that every thing which is not expressly given to Congress is reserved."

In the first place then it is most certain that we find no such clause or article in the new constitution. There is nothing in the new constitution which either in form or substance bears the least resemblance to the second article of the confederation. It might nevertheless be a fair argument to insist upon from the nature of delegated powers, that no more power is given in such cases than is expressly given. Whether or not this ground of argument would be such as we might safely rest our liberties upon; or whether it would be more prudent to stipulate expressly as is done in the present confederation for the reservation of all such powers as are not expressly given, it is hardly necessary to determine at present. It strikes me that by the proposed constitution, so far from the reservation of all powers that are not expressly given, THE FUTURE CONGRESS WILL BE FULLY AUTHORISED TO ASSUME ALL SUCH POWERS AS THEY IN THEIR WISDOM OR WICKEDNESS, ACCORDING AS THE ONE OR THE OTHER MAY HAPPEN TO PREVAIL, SHALL FROM TIME TO TIME THINK PROPER TO ASSUME.

Let us weigh this matter carefully; for it is certainly of the utmost importance, and, if I am right in my opinion, the new constitution vests Congress with such unlimited powers as ought never to be entrusted to any men or body of men. It is justly observed that the possession of sovereign power is a temptation too great for human nature to resist; and although we have read in history of one or two illustrious characters who have refused to enslave their country when it was in their power;—although we have seen one illustrious character in our own times resisting the possession of power when set in competition with his duty to his country, yet these instances are so very rare, that it would be worse than madness to trust to the chance of their being often repeated.

To proceed then with the enquiry, whether the future Congress will be restricted to those powers which are expressly given to them. I would observe that in the opinion of MONTESQUIEU, and of most other writers, ancient as well as modern, the legislature is the sovereign power. It is certainly the most important. If any one doubts this, let him reflect upon the frequent inroads which the legislature of Pennsylvania has made upon the other branches of government: Inroads which it is much to be feared, if the powers of government in Pennsylvania should ever in time to come be an object worth contending about, no council of censors will ever be able to check or restrain. Let us then see what are the powers expressly given to the legislature of Congress, and what checks are interposed in the way of the continental legislature's assuming what further power they shall think proper to assume.

To this end let us look to the first article of the proposed new constitution, which treats of the legislative powers of Congress; and to the eighth section which PRETENDS to define those powers. We find here that the congress, in its legislative capacity, shall have the power "to lay and collect taxes, duties and excises; to borrow money; to regulate commerce; to fix the rule for naturalization and the laws of bankruptcy; to coin money; to punish counterfeiters; establish post offices and post roads; to secure copy rights to authors; to constitute tribunals; to define and punish piracies; to declare war; to raise and support armies; to provide and support a navy; to make rules for the army and navy; to call forth the militia; to organize, arm and discipline the militia; to exercise absolute power over a district of ten miles square, independant of all the state legislatures, and to be alike absolute over all forts, magazines, arsenals, dockyards and other needful buildings thereunto belonging." This is a short abstract of the powers expressly given to Congress. These powers are very extensive, but I shall not stay at present to inquire whether these EXPRESS powers were necessary to be given to Congress? whether they are too great or too small? My object is to consider that UNDEFINED, UNBOUNDED AND IMMENSE POWER which is comprised in the following clause;—"And, to make all laws which shall be necessary and proper for carrying into execution the FOREGOING POWERS AND ALL OTHER POWERS vested by this constitution in the government of the United States; or in any department or offices thereof." Under such a clause as this can any thing be said to be reserved and kept back from Congress? Can it be said that the Congress have no power but what is expressed? "To make all laws which shall be necessary and proper" is in other words to make all such laws which THE CONGRESS SHALL THINK NECESSARY AND PROPER,—for who shall judge for the legislature what is necessary and proper?—Who shall set themselves above the sovereign?—What inferior legislature shall set itself above the supreme legislature?—To me it appears that no other power on earth can dictate to them or controul them, unless by force; and force either internal or external is one of those calamities which every good man would wish his country at all times to be delivered from.—This generation in America have seen enough of war and its usual concomitants to prevent all of us from wishing to see any more of it;— all except those who make a trade of war. But to the question;— without force what can restrain the Congress from making such laws as they please? What limits are there to their authority?—I fear none at all; for surely it cannot justly be said that they have no power but what is expressly given to them, whereby the very terms of their creation they are vested with the powers of making laws in all cases necessary and proper; when from the nature of their power they must necessarily be the judges, what laws are necessary and proper. The British act of Parliament, declaring the power of Parliament to make laws to bind America in all cases whatsoever, was not more extensive; for it is as true as a maxim, that even the British Parliament neither could nor would pass any law in any case in which they did not either deem it necessary and proper to make such law or pretend to deem it so. And in such cases it is not of a farthing consequence whether they really are of opinion that the law is necessary and proper, or only PRETEND TO THINK SO; for who can overrule their pretensions?-No one, unless we had a bill of rights to which we might appeal, and under which we might contend against any assumption of undue power and appeal to the judicial branch of the government to protect us by their judgements. This reasoning I fear Mr. Printer is but too just; and yet, if any man should doubt the truth of it; let me ask him one other question, what is the meaning of the latter part of the clause which vests the Congress with the authority of making all laws which shall be necessary and proper for carrying into execution ALL OTHER POWERS;-besides the foregoing powers vested, &c. &c. Was it thought that the foregoing powers might perhaps admit of some restraint in THEIR construction as to what was necessary and proper to carry them into execution? Or was it deemed right to add still further that they should not be restrained to the powers already named?—besides the powers already mentioned, other powers may be assumed hereafter as contained by implication in this constitution. The Congress shall judge of what is necessary and proper in all these cases and in all other cases;—in short in all cases whatsoever.

Where then is the restraint? How are Congress bound down to the powers expressly given? what is reserved or can be reserved?

Yet even this is not all—as if it were determined that no doubt should remain, by the sixth article of the constitution it is declared that, "this constitution, and the laws of the United States which shall be made in pursuance thereof; and all treaties made, or which shall be made, under the authority of the United States, shall be the supreme law of the land, and the judges in every state shall be bound thereby, ANY THING IN THE CONSTITUTIONS OR LAWS OF ANY STATE TO THE CONTRARY NOTWITHSTANDING." The Congress are therefore vested with the supreme legislative power, without controul. In giving such immense, such unlimited powers, was there no necessity of a bill of rights to secure to the people their liberties? Is it not evident that we are left wholly dependent on the wisdom and virtue of the men who shall from time to time be the members of Congress? and who shall be able to say seven years hence, the members of Congress will be wise and good men, or of the contrary character.

As I mean to pursue this subject in some other letters, I shall conclude for the present; and am, Yours, AN OLD WHIG.

Essays of Brutus: *Essay I*

Publication: New York Journal and Weekly Register

Date: October 18, 1787

Author: Robert Yates

To the Citizens of the State of New-York.

When the public is called to investigate and decide upon a question in which not only the present members of the community are deeply interested, but upon which the happiness and misery of generations yet unborn is in great measure suspended, the benevolent mind cannot help feeling itself peculiarly interested in the result.

In this situation, I trust the feeble efforts of an individual, to lead the minds of the people to a wise and prudent determination, cannot fail of being acceptable to the candid and dispassionate part of the community. Encouraged by this consideration, I have been induced to offer my thoughts upon the present important crisis of our public affairs.

Perhaps this country never saw so critical a period in their political concerns. We have felt the feebleness of the ties by which these United-States are held together, and the want of sufficient energy in our present confederation, to manage, in some instances, our general concerns. Various expedients have been proposed to remedy these evils, but none have succeeded. At length a Convention of the states has been assembled, they have formed a constitution which will now, probably, be submitted to the people to ratify or reject, who are the fountain of all power, to whom alone it of right belongs to make or unmake constitutions, or forms of government, at their pleasure. The most important question that was ever proposed to your decision, or to the decision of any people under heaven, is before you, and you are to decide upon it by men of your own election, chosen specially for this purpose. If the constitution, offered to [your acceptance], be a wise one, calculated to preserve the invaluable blessings of liberty, to secure the inestimable rights of mankind, and promote human happiness, then, if you accept it, you will lay a lasting foundation of happiness for millions yet unborn; generations to come will rise up and call you blessed. You may rejoice in the prospects of this vast extended continent becoming filled with freemen, who will assert the dignity of human nature. You may solace yourselves with the idea, that society, in this favoured land, will fast advance to the highest point of perfection; the human mind will expand in knowledge and virtue, and the golden age be, in some measure, realised. But if, on the other hand, this form of government contains principles that will lead to the subversion of liberty — if it tends to establish a despotism, or, what is worse, a tyrannic aristocracy; then, if you adopt it, this only remaining assylum for liberty will be [shut] up, and posterity will execrate your memory.

Momentous then is the question you have to determine, and you are called upon by every motive which should influence a noble and virtuous mind, to examine it well, and to make up a wise judgment. It is insisted, indeed, that this constitution must be received, be it ever so imperfect. If it has its defects, it is said, they can be best amended when they are experienced. But remember, when the people once part with power, they can seldom or never resume it again but by force. Many instances can be produced in which the people have voluntarily increased the powers of their rulers; but few, if any, in which rulers have willingly abridged their authority. This is a sufficient reason to induce you to be careful, in the first instance, how you deposit the powers of government.

With these few introductory remarks I shall proceed to a consideration of this constitution:

The first question that presents itself on the subject is, whether a confederated government be the best for the United States or not? Or in other words, whether the thirteen United States should be reduced to one great republic, governed by one legislature, and under the direction of one executive and judicial; or whether they should continue thirteen confederated republics, under the direction and controul of a supreme federal head for certain defined national purposes only?

This enquiry is important, because, although the government reported by the convention does not go to a perfect and entire consolidation, yet it approaches so near to it, that it must, if executed, certainly and infallibly terminate in it.

This government is to possess absolute and uncontroulable power, legislative, executive and judicial, with respect to every object to which it extends, for by the last clause of section 8th, article Ist, it is declared "that the Congress shall have power to make all laws which shall be necessary and proper for carrying into execution the foregoing powers, and all other powers vested by this constitution, in the government of the United States; or in any department or office thereof." And by the 6th article, it is declared "that this constitution, and the laws of the United States, which shall be made in pursuance thereof, and the treaties made, or which shall be made, under the authority of the United States, shall be the supreme law of the land; and the judges in every state shall be bound thereby, any thing in the constitution, or law of any state to the contrary notwithstanding." It appears from these articles that there is no need of any intervention of the state governments, between the Congress and the people, to execute any one power vested in the general government, and that the constitution and laws of every state are nullified and declared void, so far as they are or shall be inconsistent with this constitution, or the laws made in pursuance of it, or with treaties made under the authority of the United States. — The government then, so far as it extends, is a complete one, and not a confederation. It is as much one complete government as that of New-York or Massachusetts, has as absolute and perfect powers to make and execute all laws, to appoint officers, institute courts, declare offences, and annex penalties, with respect to every object to which it extends, as any other in the world. So far therefore as its powers reach, all ideas of confederation are given up and lost. It is true this government is limited to certain objects, or to speak more properly, some small degree of power is still left to the states, but a little attention to the powers vested in the general government, will convince every candid man, that if it is capable of being executed, all that is reserved for the individual states must very soon be annihilated, except so far as they are barely necessary to the organization of the general government. The powers of the general legislature extend to every case that is of the least importance — there is nothing valuable to human nature, nothing dear to freemen, but what is within its power. It has authority to make laws which will affect the lives, the liberty, and property of every man in the United States; nor can the constitution or laws of any state, in any way prevent or impede the full and complete execution of every power given. The legislative power is competent to lay taxes, duties, imposts, and excises; — there is no limitation to this power, unless it be said that the clause which directs the use to which those taxes, and duties shall be applied, may be said to be a limitation; but this is no restriction of the power at all, for by this clause they are to be applied to pay the debts and provide for the common defence and general welfare of the United States; but the legislature have authority to contract debts at their discretion; they are the sole judges of what is necessary to provide for the common defence, and they only are to determine what is for the general welfare:

this power therefore is neither more nor less, than a power to lay and collect taxes, imposts, and excises, at their pleasure; not only the power to lay taxes unlimited, as to the amount they may require, but it is perfect and absolute to raise them in any mode they please. No state legislature, or any power in the state governments, have any more to do in carrying this into effect, than the authority of one state has to do with that of another. In the business therefore of laying and collecting taxes, the idea of confederation is totally lost, and that of one entire republic is embraced. It is proper here to remark, that the authority to lay and collect taxes is the most important of any power that can be granted; it connects with it almost all other powers, or at least will in process of time draw all other after it; it is the great mean of protection, security, and defence, in a good government, and the great engine of oppression and tyranny in a bad one. This cannot fail of being the case, if we consider the contracted limits which are set by this constitution, to the late governments, on this article of raising money. No state can emit paper money — lay any duties, or imposts, on imports, or exports, but by consent of the Congress; and then the net produce shall be for the benefit of the United States. The only mean therefore left, for any state to support its government and discharge its debts, is by direct taxation; and the United States have also power to lay and collect taxes, in any way they please. Every one who has thought on the subject, must be convinced that but small sums of money can be collected in any country, by direct taxe[s], when the foederal government begins to exercise the right of taxation in all its parts, the legislatures of the several states will find it impossible to raise monies to support their governments. Without money they cannot be supported, and they must dwindle away, and, as before observed, their powers absorbed in that of the general government.

It might be here shewn, that the power in the federal legislative, to raise and support armies at pleasure, as well in peace as in war, and their controul over the militia, tend, not only to a consolidation of the government, but the destruction of liberty. — I shall not, however, dwell upon these, as a few observations upon the judicial power of this government, in addition to the preceding, will fully evince the truth of the position.

The judicial power of the United States is to be vested in a supreme court, and in such inferior courts as Congress may from time to time ordain and establish. The powers of these courts are very extensive; their jurisdiction comprehends all civil causes, except such as arise between citizens of the same state; and it extends to all cases in law and equity arising under the constitution. One inferior court must be established, I presume, in each state at least, with the necessary executive officers appendant thereto. It is easy to see, that in the common course of things, these courts will eclipse the dignity, and take away from the respectability, of the state courts. These courts will be, in themselves, totally independent of the states, deriving their authority from the United States, and receiving from them fixed salaries; and in the course of human events it is to be expected, that they will swallow up all the powers of the courts in the respective states.

How far the clause in the 8th section of the Ist article may operate to do away all idea of confederated states, and to effect an entire consolidation of the whole into one general government, it is impossible to say. The powers given by this article are very general and comprehensive, and it may receive a construction to justify the passing almost any law. A power to make all laws, which shall be NECESSARY AND PROPER, for carrying into execution, all powers vested by the constitution in the government of the United States, or any department or officer thereof, is a power very comprehensive and definite, and may, for ought I know, be exercised in a such manner as entirely to abolish the state legislatures. Suppose the legislature of a state should pass a law to raise money to support their government and pay the state debt, may the Congress repeal this law, because it may prevent the collection of a tax which they may think proper and necessary to lay, to provide for the general welfare of the United States? For all laws made, in pursuance of this constitution, are the supreme lay of the land, and the judges in every state shall be bound thereby, any thing in the constitution or laws of the different states to the contrary notwithstanding. — By such a law, the government of a particular state might be overturned at one stroke, and thereby be deprived of every means of its support.

It is not meant, by stating this case, to insinuate that the constitution would warrant a law of this kind; or unnecessarily to alarm the fears of the people, by suggesting, that the federal legislature would be more likely to pass the limits assigned them by the constitution, than that of an individual state, further than they are less responsible to the people. But what is meant is, that the legislature of the United States are vested with the great and uncontroulable powers, of laying and collecting taxes, duties, imposts, and excises; of regulating trade, raising and supporting armies, organizing, arming, and disciplining the militia, instituting courts, and other general powers. And are by this clause invested with the power of making all laws, PROPER AND NECESSARY, for carrying all these into execution; and they may so exercise this power as entirely to annihilate all the state governments, and reduce this country to one single government. And if they may do it, it is pretty certain they will; for it will be found that the power retained by individual states, small as it is, will be a clog upon the wheels of the government of the United States; the latter therefore will be naturally inclined to remove it out of the way. Besides, it is a truth confirmed by the unerring experience of ages, that every man, and every body of men, invested with power, are ever disposed to increase it, and to acquire a superiority over every thing that stands in their way. This disposition, which is implanted in human nature, will operate in the federal legislature to lessen and ultimately to subvert the state authority, and having such advantages, will most certainly succeed, if the federal government succeeds at all. It must be very evident then, that what this constitution wants of being a complete consolidation of the several parts of the union into one complete government, possessed of perfect legislative, judicial, and executive powers, to all intents and purposes, it will necessarily acquire in its exercise and operation.

Let us now proceed to enquire, as I at first proposed, whether it be best the thirteen United States should be reduced to one great republic, or not? It is here taken for granted, that all agree in this, that whatever government we adopt, it ought to be a free one; that it should be so framed as to secure the liberty of the citizens of America, and such an one as to admit of a full, fair, and equal representation of the people. The question then will be, whether a government thus constituted, and founded on such principles, is practicable, and can be exercised over the whole United States, reduced into one state?

If respect is to be paid to the opinion of the greatest and wisest men who have ever thought or wrote on the science of government, we shall be constrained to conclude, that a free republic cannot succeed over a country of such immense extent, containing such a number of inhabitants, and these encreasing in such rapid progression as that of the whole United States. Among the many illustrious authorities which might be produced to this point, I shall content myself with quoting only two. The one is the baron de Montesquieu, spirit of laws, chap. xvi. vol. I [book VIII]. "It is natural to a republic to have only a small territory, otherwise it cannot long subsist. In a large republic there are men of large fortunes, and consequently of less moderation; there are trusts too great to be placed in any single subject; he has interest of his own; he soon begins to think that he may be happy, great and glorious, by oppressing his fellow citizens; and that he may raise himself to grandeur on the ruins of his country. In a large republic, the public good is sacrificed to a thousand views; it is subordinate to exceptions, and depends on accidents. In a small one, the interest of the public is easier perceived, better understood, and more within the reach of every citizen; abuses are of less extent, and of course are less protected." Of the same opinion is the marquis Beccarari.

History furnishes no example of a free republic, any thing like the extent of the United States. The Grecian republics were of small extent; so also was that of the Romans. Both of these, it is true, in process of time, extended their conquests over large territories of country; and the consequence was, that their governments were changed from that of free governments to those of the most tyrannical that ever existed in the world.

Not only the opinion of the greatest men, and the experience of mankind, are against the idea of an extensive republic, but a variety of reasons may be drawn from the reason and nature of things, against it. In every government, the will of the sovereign is the law. In despotic governments, the supreme authority being lodged in one, his will is law, and can be as easily expressed to a large extensive territory as to a small one. In a pure democracy the people are the sovereign, and their will is declared by themselves; for this purpose they must all come together to deliberate, and decide. This kind of government cannot be exercised, therefore, over a country of any considerable extent; it must be confined to a single city, or at least limited to such bounds as that the people can conveniently assemble, be able to debate, understand the subject submitted to them, and declare their opinion concerning it.

In a free republic, although all laws are derived from the consent of the people, yet the people do not declare their consent by themselves in person, but by representatives, chosen by them, who are supposed to know the minds of their constituents, and to be possessed of integrity to declare this mind.

In every free government, the people must give their assent to the laws by which they are governed. This is the true criterion between a free government and an arbitrary one. The former are ruled by the will of the whole, expressed in any manner they may agree upon; the latter by the will of one, or a few. If the people are to give their assent to the laws, by persons chosen and appointed by them, the manner of the choice and the number chosen, must be such, as to possess, be disposed, and consequently qualified to declare the sentiments of the people; for if they do not know, or are not disposed to speak the sentiments of the people, the people do not govern, but the sovereignty is in a few. Now, in a large extended country, it is impossible to have a representation, possessing the sentiments, and of integrity, to declare the minds of the people, without having it so numerous and unwieldly, as to be subject in great measure to the inconveniency of a democratic government.

The territory of the United States is of vast extent; it now contains near three millions of souls, and is capable of containing much more than ten times that number. Is it practicable for a country, so large and so numerous as they will soon become, to elect a representation, that will speak their sentiments, without their becoming so numerous as to be incapable of transacting public business? It certainly is not.

In a republic, the manners, sentiments, and interests of the people should be similar. If this be not the case, there will be a constant clashing of opinions; and the representatives of one part will be continually striving against those of the other. This will retard the operations of government, and prevent such conclusions as will promote the public good. If we apply this remark to the condition of the United States, we shall be convinced that it forbids that we should be one government. The United States includes a variety of climates. The productions of the different parts of the union are very variant, and their interests, of consequence, diverse. Their manners and habits differ as much as their climates and productions; and their sentiments are by no means coincident. The laws and customs of the several states are, in many respects, very diverse, and in some opposite; each would be in favor of its own interests and customs, and, of consequence, a legislature, formed of representatives from the respective parts, would not only be too numerous to act with any care or decision, but would be composed of such heterogenous and discordant principles, as would constantly be contending with each other.

The laws cannot be executed in a republic, of an extent equal to that of the United States, with promptitude.

The magistrates in every government must be supported in the execution of the laws, either by an armed force, maintained at the public expence for that purpose; or by the people turning out to aid the magistrate upon his command, in case of resistance.

In despotic governments, as well as in all the monarchies of Europe, standing armies are kept up to execute the commands of the prince or the magistrate, and are employed for this purpose when occasion requires: But they have always proved the destruction of liberty, and

[are] abhorrent to the spirit of a free republic. In England, where they depend upon the parliament for their annual support, they have always been complained of as oppressive and unconstitutional, and are seldom employed in executing of the laws; never except on extraordinary occasions, and then under the direction of a civil magistrate.

A free republic will never keep a standing army to execute its laws. It must depend upon the support of its citizens. But when a government is to receive its support from the aid of the citizens, it must be so constructed as to have the confidence, respect, and affection of the people." Men who, upon the call of the magistrate, offer themselves to execute the laws, are influenced to do it either by affection to the government, or from fear; where a standing army is at hand to punish offenders, every man is actuated by the latter principle, and therefore, when the magistrate calls, will obey: but, where this is not the case, the government must rest for its support upon the confidence and respect which the people have for their government and laws. The body of the people being attached, the government will always be sufficient to support and execute its laws, and to operate upon the fears of any faction which may be opposed to it, not only to prevent an opposition to the execution of the laws themselves, but also to compel the most of them to aid the magistrate; but the people will not be likely to have such confidence in their rulers, in a republic so extensive as the United States, as necessary for these purposes. The confidence which the people have in their rulers, in a free republic, arises from their knowing them, from their being responsible to them for their conduct, and from the power they have of displacing them when they misbehave: but in a republic of the extent of this continent, the people in general would be acquainted with very few of their rulers: the people at large would know little of their proceedings, and it would be extremely difficult to change them. The people in Georgia and New-Hampshire would not know one another's mind, and therefore could not act in concert to enable them to effect a general change of representatives. The different parts of so extensive a country could not possibly be made acquainted with the conduct of their representatives, nor be informed of the reasons upon which measures were founded. The consequence will be, they will have no confidence in their legislature, suspect them of ambitious views, be jealous of every measure they adopt, and will not support the laws they pass. Hence the government will be nerveless and inefficient, and no way will be left to render it otherwise, but by establishing an armed force to execute the laws at the point of the bayonet – a government of all others the most to be dreaded.

In a republic of such vast extent as the United-States, the legislature cannot attend to the various concerns and wants of its different parts. It cannot be sufficiently numerous to be acquainted with the local condition and wants of the different districts, and if it could, it is impossible it should have sufficient time to attend to and provide for all the variety of cases of this nature, that would be continually arising.

In so extensive a republic, the great officers of government would soon become above the controul of the people, and abuse their power to the purpose of aggrandizing themselves, and oppressing them. The trust committed to the executive offices, in a country of the extent of the United-States, must be various and of magnitude. The command of all the troops and navy of the republic, the appointment of officers, the power of pardoning offences, the collecting of all the public revenues, and the power of expending them, with a number of other powers, must be lodged and exercised in every state, in the hands of a few. When these are attended with great honor and emolument, as they always will be in large states, so as greatly to interest men to pursue them, and to be proper objects for ambitious and designing men, such men will be ever restless in their pursuit after them. They will use the power, when they have acquired it, to the purposes of gratifying their own interest and ambition, and it is scarcely possible, in a very large republic, to call them to account for their misconduct, or to prevent their abuse of power.

These are some of the reasons by which it appears, that a free republic cannot long subsist over a country of the great extent of these states. If then this new constitution is calculated to consolidate the thirteen states into one, as it evidently is, it ought not to be adopted.

Though I am of opinion, that it is a sufficient objection to this government, to reject it, that it creates the whole union into one government, under the form of a republic, yet if this objection was obviated, there are exceptions to it, which are so material and fundamental, that they ought to determine every man, who is a friend to the liberty and happiness of mankind, not to adopt it. I beg the candid and dispassionate attention of my countrymen while I state these objections – they are such as have obtruded themselves upon my mind upon a careful attention to the matter, and such as I sincerely believe are well founded. There are many objections, of small moment, of which I shall take no notice – perfection is not to be expected in any thing that is the production of man – and if I did not in my conscience believe that this scheme was defective in the fundamental principles –

in the foundation upon which a free and equal government must rest –
I would hold my peace.

Essays of an Old Whig: *Essay VI*

Publication: Independent Gazetteer

Date: November 24, 1787

Author: Unknown

Mr. PRINTER, I think it is an observation of Dean Swift, that, in
political matters, all men can feel, though all cannot see. Agreeably to
this doctrine we find, that the necessity of giving additional powers to
Congress is at length FELT by all men, though it was not foreseen by a
great number of the people. As the states individually could not protect
our trade, foreign nations, friends as well as enemies, have combined
against it; and at the same time that our trade is more beneficial to any
nation in Europe, than the trade of any nation in Europe is to us,
because we export provisions and raw materials and receive
manufactures in return: we are not suffered to be the carriers of our
own produce—foreign bottoms engross the whole of our carrying
trade, and we are obliged to pay them for doing that which it is the
interest of every people to do for themselves. Our shipwrights are
starved, our seamen driven abroad for want of employ, our timber left
useless on our hands, our ironworks, once a very profitable branch of
business, now almost reduced to nothing, and our money banished
from the country. These with the train of concomitant evils which
always attend the loss of trade, or a state of trade which is unprofitable,
have justly alarmed us all; and I am firmly pursuaded that scarcely a
man of common sense can be found, that does not wish for an efficient
federal government, and lament that it has been delayed so long. Yet at
the same time it is a matter of immense consequence, in establishing a
government which is to last for ages, and which, if it be suffered to
depart from the principles of liberty in the beginning, will in all
probability, never return to them, that we consider carefully what sort
of government we are about to form. Power is very easily encreased;
indeed it naturally grows in every government; but it hardly ever
lessens.

The misfortunes under which we have for some time laboured, and
which still press us severely, would be in a great measure alleviated, if
not wholly removed, by devolving upon Congress the power of
regulating trade and laying and collecting duties and imposts. If these

powers were once fully vested in Congress, trade would immediately assume a, new face, money and people would flow in upon us, and the vast tracts of ungranted lands would be a mine of wealth for many years to come. I am pursuaded, that with this addition to the powers of Congress, we should soon find them sufficient for every purpose; and it is very certain that if we did not find them sufficient, we could easily encrease them. But instead of being contented with this, the late convention by their proposed constitution, seem to have resolved to give the new continental government every kind of power whatsoever, throughout the United States. This power I have already attempted to show, is not limited by any stipulations in favour of the liberty of the subject, and it is easy to shew, that it will be equally unchecked by any restraint from the individual states. The treasure of the whole continent will be entirely at their command. "The Congress shall have power to levy and collect taxes, duties, imposts and excises." And what are the individual states to do, or how are they to subsist? may they also lay and collect taxes, duties, imposts and excises? If they should, the miserable subject will be like sheep twice shorne; the skin must follow the fleece. But the fact is, that no individual state can collect a penny, unless by the permission of Congress; for the "laws of the United States shall be the supreme law of the land, any thing in the constitution or laws of any state to the contrary, notwithstanding." The laws of the individual states, will be only Leges sub graviore Lege: for the power of enacting laws necessarily implies the power of repealing laws; and therefore Congress, being the supreme legislatures, may annul or repeal the laws of the individual states, whenever they please. Not a single source of revenue will remain to any state, which Congress may not stop at their sovereign will and pleasure; for if any state attempt to impose a tax or levy a duty, contrary to the inclination of Congress, they have only to exert their supreme legislative power and the law imposing such tax or duty, is done away in a moment. For instance, it will very soon be found inconvenient to have two sets of excise officers in each town or county in every state, they will be in danger of clashing with each other, it will then be found "necessary and proper for carrying into execution the powers vested by the constitution in the government of the United States, or in some department or officer thereof," to forbid the individual states to levy any more excise. Congress may chuse to impose a stamp—duty. It will be very inconvenient for people to run back and forward to different offices, to procure double stamps, and therefore it will be thought "necessary and proper" to forbid any state to meddle with stamp—duties. The same will be the case with many other taxes. They will be in danger of clashing with each other, if Congress and the several states should happen to lay taxes on the same article. The States therefore individually, will be restrained from imposing any taxes upon such articles as Congress shall think proper to tax. They must then try to find out other articles for taxation, which Congress have not thought proper to touch. This I fear will be a difficult task: for the expensive court to be maintained by the great president, the pay of the standing army and the numerous crouds of hungry expectants, who have lost their all, and it will be said, have lost it by their zeal for the new constitution, must necessarily employ the sharpest wits among their ablest financiers, to devise every possible mode of taxation; and besides, if an individual state should hit upon a new tax that should happen to be productive, there is no doubt but it would soon be taken from it and appropriated to the use of the United States. The inhabitants of the TEN MILE SQUARE, would find ways and means to dispose of all the money that could possibly be raised in every part of the United States. What then will become of the separate governments? They will be annihilated; absolutely annihilated; for no man will ever submit to the wretchedness and contempt of holding any office under them.

The advocates of the proposed constitution, seem to be aware of the difficulty I have hinted at, and therefore it is, I presume, that in conversation as well as in their publications, we are told that under the pro—posed constitution, "direct taxation will be unnecessary;" that "it is probable the principal branch of revenue will be duties on imports." Some of those who have used such language in public and private, I believe to be very honest men; and I would therefore ask of them, what security they can give us, that the future government of the continent will in any measure confine themselves to the duties upon imports, or that the utmost penny will not be exacted which can possibly be collected either by direct or indirect taxation? How can they answer for the conduct of our future rulers? We have heard enough of these fair promises for the good behaviour of men in office, to learn to doubt of their fulfilment, unless we guard ourselves by much better security, there will be no bounds to the new government. They will not have as much to spare for the separate states to collect as Lazarus picked up of the frag-ments from the rich man's table; There are mouths at this moment gaping in the United States for all that can possibly be collected;—a confederacy is already formed for dividing the public cake to the last crum; and I wish they may not quarrel for more.

But if I were mistaken in this opinion; if in the language of these gentlemen, "it is probable that the principal branch of the public revenue will be duties on imports;"—if it is probable that these with the back lands and the post—office will be sufficient, where was the necessity of being in such haste to grant more;—to grant all without limits or restrictions? Men do not usually give up their whole purse where they can pay with part. Why might we not try at least how far the customs and back lands would go before we give all away from the seperate states, without reserving any thing for their support.

The true line of distinction which should have been drawn in describing the powers of Congress, and those of the several states, should have been that between internal and external taxation. I am persuaded that the existence of the several states in their separate capacities, and of the United States in their collective capacity, depends upon the maintaining such distinction. Without the power of imposing duties on foreign commerce and regulating trade, the United States will be weak and contemptible, and, indeed, their union must be speedily dissolved: And on the other hand, if the Legislature of the United States shall possess the powers of internal as well as external taxation, the individual states in their separate capacities, will be less than the shadows of a name.

I observe that the late delegates of Connecticut,— in their letter to the Governor, speak of the power of direct taxation as an authority which need not be exercised if each state will "furnish the quota." Yet there is no doubt but they may exercise this power if they choose to do it; and they alone will have the right of judging what quotas the several states shall be required to furnish. They may ask as much as they please, and if the states do not furnish all they ask, they may tax at their pleasure; under these circumstances the power of internal taxation will undoubtedly be exercised by the Continental Legislature. If it be said that it is to be expected that the Congress will exercise this power with moderation, I venture to pronounce that those who indulge such hopes, are not acquainted with the principles of human nature. Independent of the multitudinous expectations which the followers of the proposed Constitution entertain in their own favor, which alone, if gratified, would consume the treasures of two such continents as this; there is a spirit of rivalship in power, which will not suffer two suns to shine in the same firmament, one will speedily darken the other, and the individual states will be as totally eclipsed, as the stars in the meridian blaze of the sun. We have seen too much of this spirit in the several states, under the present loose and futile confederation. A jealousy of the powers of Congress in the separate states, which is founded in the same rivalship of power, and which, however contemptible it may appear, was alike founded in the principles of human nature, may furnish us an exemplary lesson upon this head: And when we verge to the other extreme by vesting all power in Congress, we shall find them equally jealous of any power in the individual states, and equally possessed of the same spirit of rivalship, which heretofore denied the necessary supplies from the states to Congress.—We shall never be able to support the collective powers of the United States in Congress, and the powers of the individual states in their separate capacities, without drawing the line fairly between them. If we leave the states individually to the mercy of the Continental Government, they will be stript of the last penny which is necessary for their support: if we give all powers to one, there will be nothing left for the others. The lust of dominion, where it is indulged, will swallow up the whole.

But I shall be told that if Congress are left to depend upon requisitions from the individual states for any part of the necessary supplies, the same difficulty will remain which has hitherto existed; and I may be asked, what shall we do if the supplies should fall short? I answer that although nothing but a very serious necessity of money for continental purposes will ever procure supplies upon requisition from the separate states, yet when that necessity exists in any degree that is really alarming to the whole community, I do not think that such supplies are to be dispaired of. We have seen many instances of aid being furnished, even voluntarily upon pressing occasions, which should teach us to rely on the exertions of the states upon occasions of real and not mere imaginary necessity. One thing will certainly follow from the Continental Governments being restrained to external taxation;— that it will be under the necessity of exercising more economy than it has done, especially during the late war. We have been witnesses of such a profuse expenditure of public money at some periods, as these states could never support. This profusion ought to convince us that if all the treasures of the continent are intrusted to the power of Congress, there is too much reason to fear that the whole will be consumed by them, and nothing left to the individual states; and judging from past experience we may venture to presage that the people will be fleeced without mercy, if no check is maintained upon the power of Congress in the articles of taxation.

We ought to be very fully convinced of an absolute necessity existing before we entrust the whole power of taxation to the hands of Congress; and the moment we do so, we ought by consent to annihilate the individual states; for the powers of the individual states will be as effectually swallowed as a drop of water in the ocean; and the next consequence will be a speedy dissolution of our republican form of government.

Letters of Centinel: *Letter V*

Publication: Independent Gazetteer

Date: December 4, 1787

Author: Samuel Bryan

To the PEOPLE of PENNSYLVANIA.

Friends, Countrymen, and Fellow-Citizens, Mr. Wilson in a speech delivered in our Convention on Saturday the 24th instant, has conceded, nay forceably proved, that one consolidated government, will not answer for so extensive a territory as the United States includes, that slavery would be the necessary fate of the people under such a government; his words are so remarkable, that I cannot forbear reciting them, they are as follows, viz. "The extent of country for which the new con- stitution was required, produced another difficulty in the business of the federal convention. It is the opinion of some celebrated writers, that to a small territory, the democratical, to a middling territory, (as Montesquieu has termed it) the monarchical, and, to an extensive territory, the despotic form of government, is best adapted. Regarding then, the wide and almost unbounded jurisdiction of the United States, at first view, the hand of despotism seemed necessary to controul, connect, and protect it; and hence the chief embarrasment rose. For, we knew that, although our constituents would chearfully submit to the legislative restraints of a free government, they would spurn at every attempt to shackle them with despotic power." See page 5 of the printed speech. And again in page 7, he says "Is it probable that the dissolution of the state governments, and the establishment of one consolidated empire, would be eligible in its nature, and satisfactory to the people in its administration? I think not, as I have given reasons to shew that so extensive a territory could not be governed, connected, and preserved, but by the supremacy of despotic power. All the exertions of the most potent emperors of Rome were not capable of keeping that empire together, which, in extent, was far inferior to the dominion of America."

This great point having been now confirmed by the concession of Mr. Wilson, though indeed it was self evident before, and the writers against the proposed plan of government, having proved to demonstration, that the powers proposed to be vested in Congress, will necessarily annihilate and absorb the state Legislatures and judiciaries and produce from their wreck one consolidated government, the question is determined. Every man therefore who has the welfare of his country at heart, every man who values his own liberty and happiness, in short, every description of persons, except those aspiring despots who hope to benefit by the mysery and vassalage of their countrymen, must now concur in rejecting the proposed system of government, must now unite in branding its authors with the stigma of eternal infamy. The anniversary of this great escape from the fangs of despotism, ought to be celebrated as long as liberty shall continue to be dear to the citizens of America.

I will repeat some of my principal arguments, and add some further remarks, on the subject consolidation.

The Legislative is the highest delegated power in government, all others are subordinate to it. The celebrated Montesquieu establishes it as a maxim, that legislation necessarily follows the power of taxation. By the 8th sect of article the 1st of the proposed government, "the Congress are to have power to lay and collect taxes, duties, imposts, and excises, to pay the debts and provide for the common defence and general welfare of the United States." Now, what can be more comprehensive than these words? Every species of taxation, whether external or internal are included. Whatever taxes, duties, and excises that the Congress may deem necessary to the general welfare may be imposed on the citizens of these states and levied by their officers. The congress are to be the absolute judges of the propriety of such taxes, in short they may construe every purpose for which the state legislatures now lay taxes, to be for the general welfare, they may seize upon every source of taxation, and thus make it impracticable for the states to have the smallest revenue, and if a state should presume to impose a tax or excise that would interfere with a federal tax or excise, congress may soon terminate the contention, by repealing the state law, by virtue of the following section—"To make all laws which shall be necessary and proper for carrying into execution the foregoing powers and all other powers vested by this constitution in the government of the United States, or in any department thereof." Indeed every law of the states may be controuled by this power. The legislative power granted for these sections is so unlimited in its nature, may be so comprehensive and boundless in its exercise, that this alone would be amply sufficient to carry the coup de grace to the state governments, to swallow them up in the grand vortex of general empire. But the legislative has an able auxiliary in the judicial department, for a reference to my second number will shew that this may be made greatly instrumental in effecting consolidation; as the federal judiciary would absorb all others. Lest the foregoing powers should not suffice to consolidate the United States into one empire, the Convention as if determined to prevent the possibility of a doubt, as if to prevent all clashing by the opposition of state powers, as if to preclude all struggle for state importance, as if to level all obstacles to the supremacy of universal sway, which in so extensive a territory, would be an iron-handed despotism, have ordained by article the 6th, "That this constitution, and the laws of the United States, which shall be made in pursuance thereof, and all treaties made, or which shall be made, under the authority of the United States, shall be the supreme law of the land and the judges in every state shall be bound thereby any thing in the constitution or laws of any state to the contrary notwithstanding."

The words "pursuant to the constitution" will be no restriction to the authority of congress; for the foregoing sections gives them unlimited legislation; their unbounded power of taxation does alone include all others, as whoever has the purse strings will have full dominion. But the convention has superadded another power, by which the congress may stamp with the sanction of the constitution every possible law; it is contained in the following clause—"To make all laws which shall be necessary and proper for carrying into execution the foregoing powers, and all other powers vested by this constitution in the government of the United States, or in any department or officer thereof " Whatever law congress may deem necessary and proper for carrying into execution any of the powers vested in them, may be enacted; and by virtue of this clause, they may controul and abrogate any and every of the laws of the state governments, on the allegation that they interfere with the execution of any of their powers, and yet these laws will "be made in pursuance of the constitution," and of course will "be the supreme law of the land, and the judges in every state shall be bound thereby, any thing in the constitution or laws of any state to the contrary notwithstanding."

There is no reservation made in the whole of this plan in favor of the rights of the separate states. In the present plan confederation made in the year 1778, it was thought necessary by article the 2d to declare that "each state retains its sovereignty, freedom and independence, and every power, jurisdiction and right, which is not by this confederation expressly delegated to the United States in Congress assembled." Positive grant was not then thought sufficiently descriptive and restrictive upon congress, and the omission of such a declaration now, when such great devolutions of power are proposed, manifests the design of consolidating the states.

What restriction does Mr. Wilson pretend there is in the new constitution to the supremacy of despotic sway over the United States? What barrier does he assign for the security of the state governments? Why truly a mere cobweb of a limit! by interposing the shield of what will become mere form, to check the reality of power. He says, that the existence of the state governments are essential to the organization of congress, that the former is made the necessary basis of the latter, for the federal senators and president are to be appointed by the state legislatures; and that hence all fears of a consolidation are groundless and imaginary. It must be confessed, as reason and argument would have been foreign to the defence of the proposed plan of government, Mr. Wilson has displayed much ingenuity on this occasion, he has involved the subject in all the mazes of sophistry, and by subtil distinctions, he has established principles and positions, that exist only in his own fertile imagination. It is a solecism in politics for two coordinate sovereignties to exist together, you must separate the sphere of their jurisdiction, or after running the race of dominion for some time, one would necessarily triumph over the other; but in the mean time the subjects of it would be harrassed with double impositions to support the contention; however the strife between congress and the states could not be of long continuance, for the former has a decisive superiority in the outset, and has moreover the power by the very constitution itself to terminate it, when expedient.

As this necessary connexion, as it has been termed, between the state governments and the general government, has been made a point of great magnitude by the advocates of the new plan, as it is the only obstacle alledged by them against a consolidation, it ought to be well considered. It is declared by the proposed plan, that the federal senators and the electors who chuse the president of the United States, shall be appointed by the state legislatures for the long period of six and four years respectively;—how will this connexion prevent the state legislatures being divested of every important, every efficient power? may not they, will not they dwindle into mere boards appointment, as has ever happened in other nations to public bodies, who, in similar circumstances, have been so weak as to part with the essentials of power? Does not history abound with such instances? And this may be the mighty amount of this inseparable connexion, which is so much dwelt upon as the security of the state governments. Yet even this shadow of a limit against consolidation, may be annihilated by the imperial fiat, without any violation of even the forms of the constitution, section 4th of article the 1st has made a provision for this, when the people are sufficiently fatigued with the useless expence maintaining the forms of departed power and security, and when they shall pray to be relieved from the imposition. This section cannot be too often repeated, as it gives such a latitude to the designing, as it revoke's every other part of the constitution that may be tolerable, and as it may enable the administration under it, to complete the system of despotism; it is in the following words, viz. "The times, places and manner of holding elections for senators and representatives, shall be prescribed in each state by the legislature thereof; but the Congress may at any time by law make or alter such regulations, except as to the place of chusing senators." The only apparent restriction in this clause, is as to the place of appointing senators, but even this may be rendered of no avail, for as the Congress have the controul over the time appointment of both senators and representatives, they may under the pretence of an apprehension of invasion, upon the pretence of the turbulence of what they may stile a faction, and indeed pretences are never wanting to the designing, they may postpone the time of the election of the senators and the representatives from period to period to perpetuity; thus they may and if they may, they certainly will from the lust of dominion, so inherent in the mind of man, relieve the people from the trouble of attending elections condescending to create themselves. Has not Mr. Wilson avowed it in fact? Has he not said in the Convention, that it was necessary that Congress should possess this power as the means of its own preservation, otherwise says he, an invasion, a civil war, a faction, or a secession of a minority of the assembly might prevent the representation of a state in Congress.

The advocates of the proposed government must be hard driven, when they represent, that because the legislatures of this and the other states have exceeded the due bounds of power, notwithstanding every guard provided by their constitutions; that because the lust of arbitrary sway is so powerful as sometimes to get the better of every obstacle; that therefore we should give full scope to it, for that all restriction would be useless and nugatory. And further, when they tell you that a good administration will atone for all the defects in the government, which, say they, you must necessarily have, for how can it be otherwise, your rulers are to be taken from among yourselves. My fellow citizens, these aspiring despots, must indeed have a great contempt for your understandings, when they hope to gull you out of your liberties by such reasoning; for what is the primary object of government, but to check and controul the ambitious and designing, how then can moderation and virtue be expected from men, who will be in possession of absolute sway, who will have the United States at their disposal? They would be more than men, who could resist such temptation! their being taken from among the people, would be no security; tyrants are of native growth in all countries, the greatest bashaw in Turky has been one of the people, as Mr. Wilson tells you the president general be. What consolation would this be, when you shall be suffering under his oppression.

Essays of Brutus: *Essay XII*

Publication: New York Journal and Weekly Register

Date: February 7, 1788

Author: Robert Yates

In my last, I shewed, that the judicial power of the United States under the first clause of the second section of article eight, would be authorized to explain the constitution, not only according to its letter, but according to its spirit and intention; and having this power, they would strongly incline to give it such a construction as to extend the powers of the general government, as much as possible, to the diminution, and finally to the destruction, of that of the respective states.

I shall now proceed to shew how this power will operate in its exercise to effect these purposes. In order to perceive the extent of its influence, I shall consider,

First. How it will tend to extend the legislative authority.

Second. In what manner it will increase the jurisdiction of the courts, and

Third. The way in which it will diminish, and destroy, both the legislative and judicial authority of the United States.

First. Let us enquire how the judicial power will effect an extension of the legislative authority.

Perhaps the judicial power will not be able, by direct and positive decrees, ever to direct the legislature, because it is not easy to conceive how a question can be brought before them in a course of legal discussion, in which they can give a decision, declaring, that the legislature have certain powers which they have not exercised, and which, in consequence of the determination of the judges, they will be bound to exercise. But it is easy to see, that in their adjudications they may establish certain principles, which being received by the legislature, will enlarge the sphere of their power beyond all bounds.

It is to be observed, that the supreme court has the power, in the last resort, to determine all questions that may arise in the course of legal discussion, on the meaning and construction of the constitution. This power they will hold under the constitution, and independent of the legislature. The latter can no more deprive the former of this right, than either of them, or both of them together, can take from the president, with the advice of the senate, the power of making treaties, or appointing ambassadors.

In determining these questions, the court must and will assume certain principles, from which they will reason, in forming their decisions. These principles, whatever they may be, when they become fixed, by a course of decisions, will be adopted by the legislature, and will be the rule by which they will explain their own powers. This appears evident from this consideration, that if the legislature pass laws, which, in the judgment of the court, they are not authorised to do by the constitution, the court will not take notice of them; for it will not be denied, that the constitution is the highest or supreme law. And the courts are vested with the supreme and uncontroulable power, to determine, in all cases that come before them, what the constitution means; they cannot, therefore, execute a law, which, in their judgment, opposes the constitution, unless we can suppose they can make a superior law give way to an inferior. The legislature, therefore, will not go over the limits by which the courts may adjudge they are confined. And there is little room to doubt but that they will come up to those bounds, as often as occasion and opportunity may offer, and they may judge it proper to do it. For as on the one hand, they will not readily pass laws which they know the courts will not execute, so on the other, we may be sure they will not scruple to pass such as they know they will give effect, as often as they may judge it proper.

From these observations it appears, that the judgment of the judicial, on the constitution, will become the rule to guide the legislature in their construction of their powers.

What the principles are, which the courts will adopt, it is impossible for us to say; but taking up the powers as I have explained them in my last number, which they will possess under this clause, it is not difficult to see, that they may, and probably will, be very liberal ones.

We have seen, that they will be authorized to give the constitution a construction according to its spirit and reason, and not to confine themselves to its letter.

To discover the spirit of the constitution, it is of the first importance to attend to the principal ends and designs it has in view. These are expressed in the preamble, in the following words, viz. "We, the people of the United States, in order to form a more perfect union, establish justice, insure domestic tranquility, provide for the common defence, promote the general welfare, and secure the blessings of liberty to ourselves and our posterity, do ordain and establish this constitution," &c. If the end of the government is to be learned from these words, which are clearly designed to declare it, it is obvious it has in view every object which is embraced by any government. The preservation of internal peace—the due administration of justice—and to provide for the defence of the community, seems to include all the objects of government; but if they do not, they are certainly comprehended in the words, "to provide for the general welfare." If it be further considered, that this constitution, if it is ratified, will not be a compact entered into by states, in their corporate capacities, but an agreement of the people of the United States, as one great body politic, no doubt can remain, but that the great end of the constitution, if it is to be collected from the preamble, in which its end is declared, is to constitute a government which is to extend to every case for which any government is instituted, whether external or internal. The courts, therefore, will establish this as a principle in expounding the constitution, and will give every part of it such an explanation, as will give latitude to every department under it, to take cognizance of every matter, not only that affects the general and national concerns of the union, but also of such as relate to the administration of private justice, and to regulating the internal and local affairs of the different parts.

Such a rule of exposition is not only consistent with the general spirit of the preamble, but it will stand confirmed by considering more minutely the different clauses of it.

The first object declared to be in view is, "To form a perfect union." It is to be observed, it is not an union of states or bodies corporate; had this been the case the existence of the state governments, might have been secured. But it is a union of the people of the United States considered as one body, who are to ratify this constitution, if it is adopted. Now to make a union of this kind perfect, it is necessary to abolish all inferior governments, and to give the general one compleat legislative, executive and judicial powers to every purpose. The courts therefore will establish it as a rule in explaining the constitution to give it such a construction as will best tend to perfect the union or take from the state governments every power of either making or executing laws. The second object is "to establish justice." This must include not only the idea of instituting the rule of justice, or of making laws which shall be the measure or rule of right, but also of providing for the application of this rule or of administering justice under it. And under this the courts will in their decisions extend the power of the government to all cases they possibly can, or otherwise they will be restricted in doing what appears to be the intent of the constitution they should do, to wit, pass laws and provide for the execution of them, for the general distribution of justice between man and man. Another end declared is "to insure domestic tranquility." This comprehends a provision against all private breaches of the peace, as well as against all public commotions or general insurrections; and to attain the object of this clause fully, the government must exercise the power of passing laws on these subjects, as well as of appointing magistrates with authority to execute them. And the courts will adopt these ideas in their expositions. I might proceed to the other clause, in the preamble, and it would appear by a consideration of all of them separately, as it does by taking them together, that if the spirit of this system is to be known from its declared end and design in the preamble, its spirit is to subvert and abolish all the powers of the state government, and to embrace every object to which any government extends.

As it sets out in the preamble with this declared intention, so it proceeds in the different parts with the same idea. Any person, who will peruse the 8th section with attention, in which most of the powers are enumerated, will perceive that they either expressly or by implication extend to almost every thing about which any legislative power can be employed. But if this equitable mode of construction is applied to this part of the constitution; nothing can stand before it.

This will certainly give the first clause in that article a construction which I confess I think the most natural and grammatical one, to authorise the Congress to do any thing which in their judgment will tend to provide for the general welfare, and this amounts to the same thing as general and unlimited powers of legislation in all cases.

(TO BE CONTINUED.)

5

BILL OF RIGHTS
Ratified December 15, 1791

Amendment I: Congress shall make no law respecting an establishment of religion, or prohibiting the free exercise thereof; or abridging the freedom of speech, or of the press; or the right of the people peaceably to assemble, and to petition the Government for a redress of grievances.

Amendment II: A well regulated Militia, being necessary to the security of a free State, the right of the people to keep and bear Arms, shall not be infringed.

Amendment III: No Soldier shall, in time of peace be quartered in any house, without the consent of the Owner, nor in time of war, but in a manner to be prescribed by law.

Amendment IV: The right of the people to be secure in their persons, houses, papers, and effects, against unreasonable searches and seizures, shall not be violated, and no Warrants shall issue, but upon probable cause, supported by Oath or affirmation, and particularly describing the place to be searched, and the persons or things to be seized.

Amendment V: No person shall be held to answer for a capital, or otherwise infamous crime, unless on a presentment or indictment of a Grand Jury, except in cases arising in the land or naval forces, or in the Militia, when in actual service in time of War or public danger; nor shall any person be subject for the same offence to be twice put in jeopardy of life or limb; nor shall be compelled in any criminal case to be a witness against himself, nor be deprived of life, liberty, or property, without due process of law; nor shall private property be taken for public use, without just compensation.

Amendment VI: In all criminal prosecutions, the accused shall enjoy the right to a speedy and public trial, by an impartial jury of the State and district wherein the crime shall have been committed, which district shall have been previously ascertained by law, and to be informed of the nature and cause of the accusation; to be confronted with the witnesses against him; to have compulsory process for obtaining witnesses in his favor, and to have the Assistance of Counsel for his defence.

Amendment VII: In Suits at common law, where the value in controversy shall exceed twenty dollars, the right of trial by jury shall be preserved, and no fact tried by a jury, shall be otherwise re-examined in any Court of the United States, than according to the rules of the common law.

Amendment VIII: Excessive bail shall not be required, nor excessive fines imposed, nor cruel and unusual punishments inflicted.

Amendment IX: The enumeration in the Constitution, of certain rights, shall not be construed to deny or disparage others retained by the people.

Amendment X: The powers not delegated to the United States by the Constitution, nor prohibited by it to the States, are reserved to the States respectively, or to the people.

6

TEN SUPREME COURT CASES ON THE RELATIONSHIP BETWEEN THE FEDERAL GOVERNMENT AND THE STATES

For ease of reading, internal citations have been omitted from the quotations. To read each case, please visit www.supreme.justia.com or www.findlaw.com/casecode/supreme.html.

1. McCulloch v. Maryland, 17 U.S. 4 Wheat. 316, 413-415 (1819)

"But the argument on which most reliance is placed is drawn from that peculiar language of this clause. Congress is not empowered by it to make all laws which may have relation to the powers conferred on the Government, but such only as may be "necessary and proper" for carrying them into execution. The word "necessary" is considered as controlling the whole sentence, and as limiting the right to pass laws for the execution of the granted powers to such as are indispensable, and without which the power would be nugatory. That it excludes the choice of means, and leaves to Congress in each case that only which is most direct and simple.

Is it true that this is the sense in which the word "necessary" is always used? Does it always import an absolute physical necessity so strong that one thing to which another may be termed necessary cannot exist without that other? We think it does not. If reference be had to its use in the common affairs of the world or in approved authors, we find that it frequently imports no more than that one thing is convenient, or useful, or essential to another. To employ the means necessary to an end is generally understood as employing any means calculated to produce the end, and not as being confined to those single means without which the end would be entirely unattainable. Such is the character of human language that no word conveys to the mind in all situations one single definite idea, and nothing is more common than to use words in a figurative sense. Almost all compositions contain words which, taken in a their rigorous sense, would convey a meaning different from that which is obviously intended. It is essential to just construction that many words which import something excessive should be understood in a more mitigated sense -- in that sense which common usage justifies. The word "necessary" is of this description. It has not a fixed character peculiar to itself. It admits of all degrees of comparison, and is often connected with other words which increase or diminish the impression the mind receives of the urgency it imports. A thing may be necessary, very necessary, absolutely or indispensably necessary. To no mind would the same idea be conveyed by these several phrases. The comment on the word is well illustrated by the passage cited at the bar from the 10th section of the 1st article of the Constitution. It is, we think, impossible to compare the sentence which prohibits a State from laying "imposts, or duties on imports or exports, except what may be absolutely necessary for executing its inspection laws," with that which authorizes Congress "to make all laws which shall be necessary and proper for carrying into execution" the powers of the General Government without feeling a conviction that the convention understood itself to change materially the meaning of the word "necessary," by prefixing the word "absolutely." This word, then, like others, is used in various senses, and, in its construction, the subject, the context, the intention of the person using them are all to be taken into view.

Let this be done in the case under consideration. The subject is the execution of those great powers on which the welfare of a Nation essentially depends. It must have been the intention of those who gave these powers to insure, so far as human prudence could insure, their beneficial execution. This could not be done by confiding the choice of means to such narrow limits as not to leave it in the power of Congress to adopt any which might be appropriate, and which were conducive to the end. This provision is made in a Constitution intended to endure for ages to come, and consequently to be adapted to the various crises of human affairs. To have prescribed the means by which Government should, in all future time, execute its powers would have been to change entirely the character of the instrument and give it the properties of a legal code. It would have been an unwise attempt to provide by immutable rules for exigencies which, if foreseen at all, must have been seen dimly, and which can be best provided for as they occur. To have declared that the best means shall not be used, but those alone without which the power given would be nugatory, would have been to deprive the legislature of the capacity to avail itself of experience, to exercise its reason, and to accommodate its legislation to circumstances."

2. Gibbons v. Ogden, 22 U.S. 1, 209-211 (1824)

"Since, however, in exercising the power of regulating their own purely internal affairs, whether of trading or police, the States may sometimes enact laws, the validity of which depends on their interfering with, and being contrary to, an act of Congress passed in pursuance of the constitution, the Court will enter upon the inquiry, whether the laws of New-York, as expounded by the highest tribunal of that State, have, in their application to this case, come into collision with an act of Congress, and deprived a citizen of a right to which that act entitles him. Should this collision exist, it will be immaterial whether those laws were passed in virtue of a concurrent power 'to regulate commerce with foreign nations and among the several States,' or, in virtue of a power to regulate their domestic trade and police. In one case and the other, the acts of New-York must yield to the law of Congress; and the decision sustaining the privilege they confer, against a right given by a law of the Union, must be erroneous.

This opinion has been frequently expressed in this Court, and is founded, as well on the nature of the government as on the words of the constitution. In argument, however, it has been contended, that if a law passed by a State, in the exercise of its acknowledged sovereignty, comes into conflict with a law passed by Congress in pursuance of the constitution, they affect the subject, and each other, like equal opposing powers.

But the framers of our constitution foresaw this state of things, and provided for it, by declaring the supremacy not only of itself, but of the laws made in pursuance of it. The nullity of any act, law. The appropriate inconsistent with the constitution, is produced by the declaration, that the constitution is the supreme law. The appropriate application of that part of the clause which confers the same supremacy on laws and treaties, is to such acts of the State Legislatures as do not transcend their powers, but, though enacted in the execution of acknowledged State powers, interfere with, or are contrary to the laws of Congress, made in pursuance of the constitution, or some treaty made under the authority of the United States. In every such case, the act of Congress, or the treaty, is supreme; and the law of the State, though enacted in the exercise of powers not controverted, must yield to it."

3. Shreveport Rate Cases, 234 U.S. 342, 353-354 (1914)

"While these decisions sustaining the Federal power relate to measures adopted in the interest of the safety of persons and property, they illustrate the principle that Congress, in the exercise of its paramount power, may prevent the common instrumentalities of interstate and intrastate commercial intercourse from being used in their intrastate operations to the injury of interstate commerce. This is not to say that Congress possesses the authority to regulate the internal commerce of a state, as such, but that it does possess the power to foster and protect interstate commerce, and to take all measures necessary or appropriate to that end, although intrastate transactions of interstate carriers may thereby be controlled.

This principle is applicable here. We find no reason to doubt that Congress is entitled to keep the highways of interstate communication open to interstate traffic upon fair and equal terms. That an unjust discrimination in the rates of a common carrier, by which one person or locality is unduly favored as against another under substantially similar conditions of traffic, constitutes an evil, is undeniable; and where this evil consists in the action of an interstate carrier in unreasonably discriminating against interstate traffic over its line, the authority of Congress to prevent it is equally clear. It is immaterial, so far as the protecting power of Congress is concerned, that the discrimination arises from intrastate rates as compared with interstate rates. The use of the instrument of interstate commerce in a discriminatory manner so as to inflict injury upon that commerce, or some part thereof, furnishes abundant ground for Federal intervention. Nor can the attempted exercise of state authority alter the matter, where Congress has acted, for a state may not authorize the carrier to do that which Congress is entitled to forbid and has forbidden."

4. A.L.A. Schechter Poultry Corp. v. United States, 295 U.S. 495, 548-550 (1935)

"While these decisions related to the application of the federal statute, and not to its constitutional validity, the distinction between direct and indirect effects of intrastate transactions upon interstate commerce must be recognized as a fundamental one, essential to the maintenance of our constitutional system. Otherwise, as we have said, there would be virtually no limit to the federal power, and, for all practical purposes, we should have a completely centralized government. We must consider the provisions here in question in the light of this distinction.

The question of chief importance relates to the provisions of the Code as to the hours and wages of those employed in defendants' slaughterhouse markets. It is plain that these requirements are imposed in order to govern the details of defendants' management of their local business. The persons employed in slaughtering and selling in local trade are not employed in interstate commerce. Their hours and wages have no direct relation to interstate commerce. The question of how many hours these employees should work and what they should be paid differs in no essential respect from similar questions in other local businesses which handle commodities brought into a State and there dealt in as a part of its internal commerce. This appears from an examination of the considerations urged by the Government with respect to conditions in the poultry trade. Thus, the Government argues that hours and wages affect prices; that slaughterhouse men sell at a small margin above operating costs; that labor represents 50 to 60 percent of these costs; that a slaughterhouse operator paying lower wages or reducing his cost by exacting long hours of work translates his saving into lower prices; that this results in demands for a cheaper grade of goods, and that the cutting of prices brings about a demoralization of the price structure. Similar conditions may be adduced in relation to other businesses. The argument of the Government proves too much. If the federal government may determine the wages and hours of employees in the internal commerce of a State, because of their relation to cost and prices and their indirect effect upon interstate commerce, it would seem that a similar control might be exerted over other elements of cost also affecting prices, such as the number of employees, rents, advertising, methods of doing business, etc. All the processes of production and distribution that enter into cost could likewise be controlled. If the cost of doing an intrastate business is, in itself, the permitted object of federal control, the extent of the regulation of cost would be a question of discretion, and not of power.

The Government also makes the point that efforts to enact state legislation establishing high labor standards have been impeded by the belief that, unless similar action is taken generally, commerce will be diverted from the States adopting such standards, and that this fear of diversion has led to demands for federal legislation on the subject of wages and hours. The apparent implication is that the federal authority under the commerce clause should be deemed to extend to the establishment of rules to govern wages and hours in intrastate trade and industry generally throughout the country, thus overriding the authority of the States to deal with domestic problems arising from labor conditions in their internal commerce.

It is not the province of the Court to consider the economic advantages or disadvantage of such a centralized system. It is sufficient to say that the Federal Constitution does not provide for it. Our growth and development have called for wide use of the commerce power of the federal government in its control over the expanded activities of interstate commerce, and in protecting that commerce from burdens, interferences, and conspiracies to restrain and monopolize it. But the authority of the federal government may not be pushed to such an extreme as to destroy the distinction, which the commerce clause itself establishes, between commerce "among the several States" and the internal concerns of a State. The same answer must be made to the contention that is based upon the serious economic situation which led to the passage of the Recovery Act -- the fall in prices, the decline in wages and employment, and the curtailment of the market for commodities. Stress is laid upon the great importance of maintaining wage distributions which would provide the necessary stimulus in starting "the cumulative forces making for expanding commercial activity." Without in any way disparaging this motive, it is enough to say that the recuperative efforts of the federal government must be made in a manner consistent with the authority granted by the Constitution.

We are of the opinion that the attempt, through the provisions of the Code, to fix the hours and wages of employees of defendants in their intrastate business was not a valid exercise of federal power."

5. N.L.R.B. v. Jones & Laughlin Steel Corp., 301 U.S. 1, 36-37 (1937)

"The congressional authority to protect interstate commerce from burdens and obstructions is not limited to transactions which can be deemed to be an essential part of a "flow" of interstate or foreign commerce. Burdens and obstructions may be due to injurious action springing from other sources. The fundamental principle is that the power to regulate commerce is the power to enact "all appropriate legislation" for "its protection and advancement"; to adopt measures "to promote its growth and insure its safety"; "to foster, protect, control and restrain." That power is plenary, and may be exerted to protect interstate commerce "no matter what the source of the dangers which threaten it." Although activities may be intrastate in character when separately considered, if they have such a close and substantial relation to interstate commerce that their control is essential or appropriate to protect that commerce from burdens and obstructions, Congress cannot be denied the power to exercise that control. Undoubtedly the scope of this power must be considered in the light of our dual system of government, and may not be extended so as to embrace effects upon interstate commerce so indirect and remote that to embrace them, in view of our complex society, would effectually obliterate the distinction between what is national and what is local and create a completely centralized government. The question is necessarily one of degree."

6. United States v. Darby, 312 U.S. 100, 115, 121 (1941)

"The motive and purpose of the present regulation are plainly to make effective the Congressional conception of public policy that interstate commerce should not be made the instrument of competition in the distribution of goods produced under substandard labor conditions, which competition is injurious to the commerce and to the states from and to which the commerce flows. The motive and purpose of a regulation of interstate commerce are matters for the legislative judgment upon the exercise of which the Constitution places no restriction, and over which the courts are given no control. "The judicial cannot prescribe to the legislative department of the government limitations upon the exercise of its acknowledged power." Whatever their motive and purpose, regulations of commerce which do not infringe some constitutional prohibition are within the plenary power conferred on Congress by the Commerce Clause. Subject only to that limitation, presently to be considered, we conclude that the prohibition of the shipment interstate of goods produced under the forbidden substandard labor conditions is within the constitutional authority of Congress.

...

Congress having by the present Act adopted the policy of excluding from interstate commerce all goods produced for the commerce which do not conform to the specified labor standards, it may choose the means reasonably adapted to the attainment of the permitted end even though they involve control of intrastate activities. Such legislation has often been sustained with respect to powers other than the commerce power granted to the national government when the means chosen, although not themselves within the granted power, were nevertheless deemed appropriate aids to the accomplishment of some purpose within an admitted power of the national government."

7. Wickard v. Filburn, 317 U.S. 111, 127-129 (1942)

"The maintenance by government regulation of a price for wheat undoubtedly can be accomplished as effectively by sustaining or increasing the demand as by limiting the supply. The effect of the statute before us is to restrict the amount which may be produced for market and the extent, as well, to which one may forestall resort to the market by producing to meet his own needs. That appellee's own contribution to the demand for wheat may be trivial by itself is not enough to remove him from the scope of federal regulation where, as here, his ontribution, taken together with that of many others similarly situated, is far from trivial.

It is well established by decisions of this Court that the power to regulate commerce includes the power to regulate the prices at which commodities in that commerce are dealt in and practices affecting such prices. One of the primary purposes of the Act in question was to increase the market price of wheat, and, to that end, to limit the volume thereof that could affect the market. It can hardly be denied that a factor of such volume and variability as home-consumed wheat would have a substantial influence on price and market conditions. This may arise because being in marketable condition such wheat overhangs the market, and, if induced by rising prices, tends to flow into the market and check price increases. But if we assume that it is never marketed, it supplies a need of the man who grew it which would otherwise be reflected by purchases in the open market. Home-grown wheat in this sense competes with wheat in commerce. The stimulation of commerce is a use of the regulatory function quite as definitely as prohibitions or restrictions thereon. This record leaves us in no doubt that Congress may properly have considered that wheat consumed on the farm where grown, if wholly outside the scheme of regulation, would have a substantial effect in defeating and obstructing its purpose to stimulate trade therein at increased prices.

It is said, however, that this Act, forcing some farmers into the market to buy what they could provide for themselves, is an unfair promotion of the markets and prices of specializing wheat growers. It is of the essence of regulation that it lays a restraining hand on the self-interest of the regulated, and that advantages from the regulation commonly fall to others. The conflicts of economic interest between the regulated and those who advantage by it are wisely left under our system to resolution by the Congress under its more flexible and responsible legislative process. Such conflicts rarely lend themselves to judicial determination. And with the wisdom, workability, or fairness, of the plan of regulation, we have nothing to do."

8. United State v. Lopez, 514 U.S. 549, 567-568 (1995)

"The possession of a gun in a local school zone is in no sense an economic activity that might, through repetition elsewhere, substantially affect any sort of interstate commerce. Respondent was a local student at a local school; there is no indication that he had recently moved in interstate commerce, and there is no requirement that his possession of the firearm have any concrete tie to interstate commerce.

To uphold the Government's contentions here, we would have to pile inference upon inference in a manner that would bid fair to convert congressional authority under the Commerce Clause to a general police power of the sort retained by the States. Admittedly, some of our prior cases have taken long steps down that road, giving great deference to congressional action. The broad language in these opinions has suggested the possibility of additional expansion, but we decline here to proceed any further. To do so would require us to conclude that the Constitution's enumeration of powers does not presuppose something not enumerated, and that there never will be a distinction between what is truly national and what is truly local. This we are unwilling to do."

9. United States v. Morrison, 529 U.S. 598, 617-618 (2000)

"We accordingly reject the argument that Congress may regulate noneconomic, violent criminal conduct based solely on that conduct's aggregate effect on interstate commerce. The Constitution requires a distinction between what is truly national and what is truly local. In recognizing this fact we preserve one of the few principles that has been consistent since the Clause was adopted. The regulation and punishment of intrastate violence that is not directed at the instrumentalities, channels, or goods involved in interstate commerce has always been the province of the States. Indeed, we can think of no better example of the police power, which the Founders denied the National Government and reposed in the States, than the suppression of violent crime and vindication of its victims.

10. N.F.I.B. v. Sebelius, 567 U.S. ___, ___ (2012)

"The Constitution grants Congress the power to "regulate Commerce." The power to regulate commerce presupposes the existence of commercial activity to be regulated. If the power to "regulate" something included the power to create it, many of the provisions in the Constitution would be superfluous.

…

The individual mandate, however, does not regulate existing commercial activity. It instead compels individuals to become active in commerce by purchasing a product, on the ground that their failure to do so affects interstate commerce. Construing the Commerce Clause to permit Congress to regulate individuals precisely because they are doing nothing would open a new and potentially vast domain to congressional authority. Every day individuals do not do an infinite number of things. In some cases they decide not to do something; in others they simply fail to do it. Allowing Congress to justify federal regulation by pointing to the effect of inaction on commerce would bring countless decisions an individual could potentially make within the scope of federal regulation, and—under the Government's theory—empower Congress to make those decisions for him.

…

The Government's theory here would effectively override that limitation, by establishing that individuals may be regulated under the Commerce Clause whenever enough of them are not doing something the Government would have them do. Indeed, the Government's logic would justify a mandatory purchase to solve almost any problem.

…

Under the Government's logic, that authorizes Congress to use its commerce power to compel citizens to act as the Government would have them act. That is not the country the Framers of our Constitution envisioned. James Madison explained that the Commerce Clause was "an addition which few oppose and from which no apprehensions are entertained." While Congress's authority under the Commerce Clause has of course expanded with the growth of the national economy, our cases have "always recognized that the power to regulate commerce, though broad indeed, has limits." The Government's theory would erode those limits, permitting Congress to reach beyond the natural extent of its authority, "everywhere extending the sphere of its activity and drawing all power into its impetuous vortex." Congress already enjoys vast power to regulate much of what we do. Accepting the Government's theory would give Congress the same license to regulate what we do not do, fundamentally changing the relation between the citizen and the Federal Government.

To an economist, perhaps, there is no difference between activity and inactivity; both have measurable economic effects on commerce. But the distinction between doing something and doing nothing would not have been lost on the Framers, who were "practical statesmen," not metaphysical philosophers. As we have explained, "the framers of the Constitution were not mere visionaries, toying with speculations or theories, but practical men, dealing with the facts of political life as they understood them, putting into form the government they were creating, and prescribing in language clear and intelligible the powers that government was to take." The Framers gave Congress the power to regulate commerce, not to compel it, and for over 200 years both our decisions and Congress's actions have reflected this understanding. There is no reason to depart from that understanding now.

...

The Commerce Clause is not a general license to regulate an individual from cradle to grave, simply because he will predictably engage in particular transactions. Any police power to regulate individuals as such, as opposed to their activities, remains vested in the States."

OTHER RESOURCES

The Federalist Papers

Federalist No. 10
Federalist No. 14
Federalist No. 17
Federalist No. 32
Federalist No. 46
Federalist No. 55
Federalist No. 62
Federalist No. 78
Federalist No. 84

The Anti-Federalist Papers

Letters from Cato: Essay III
Letters from a Federal Farmer: Essay III
Letters from a Federal Farmer: Essay IV
Letters from a Federal Farmer: Essay XVI
Letters from a Federal Farmer: Essay XVII
Letters of Brutus: Essay II
Letters of Brutus: Essay V
Letters of Brutus: Essay VI
Letters of Brutus: Essay XI

ACKNOWLEDGEMENTS

As always, a special thank you to my wife Jessica and kids for their unwavering support of my work.

Next, thank you to Mary McCleary for her assistance in editing this book and to John Fleming for his cover design work.

Finally, thank you to Michael Carnuccio for giving me the luxury of time to put together this short book on such a big issue.

ABOUT THE AUTHOR

Matt A. Mayer is the President of Opportunity Ohio (www.opportunityohio.org) and the Chief Operating Officer of The Liberty Foundation of America (www.libertyfound.org). Previously, Mayer served as a Visiting Fellow at The Heritage Foundation where he wrote extensively on the issue of federalism as it relates to national security. Mayer was a 2007 Lincoln Fellow with The Claremont Institute for the Study of Statesmanship and Political Philosophy and a 2006 American Marshall Memorial Fellow with the German Marshall Fund of the United States.

Mayer graduated from the University of Dayton with a double major in Philosophy and Psychology and received his law degree from The Ohio State University Moritz College of Law. Mayer resides in Dublin, Ohio, with his wife and three children.

www.ingramcontent.com/pod-product-compliance
Lightning Source LLC
Chambersburg PA
CBHW070748290526
45795CB00002B/527